BOUDICCA

IN SEARCH OF THE DEFILE

By

PETER SWEENEY

MAPLE
PUBLISHERS

Boudicca-In Search of the Defile

Author: Peter Sweeney

Copyright © Peter Sweeney (2023)

The right of Peter Sweeney to be identified as author of this work has been asserted by the author in accordance with section 77 and 78 of the Copyright, Designs and Patents Act 1988.

First published in 2023.

ISBN 978-1-83538-121-2 (Paperback)
 978-1-83538-122-9 (Hardback)
 978-1-83538-123-6 (E-Book)

Book Cover Design and Layout by:
 White Magic Studios
 www.whitemagicstudios.co.uk

Published by:
 Maple Publishers
 Fairbourne Drive, Atterbury,
 Milton Keynes,
 MK10 9RG, UK
 www.maplepublishers.com

To my wife Suzanne

Contents

1

Introduction

The subject of the Roman occupation of Britain has captivated the British people for generations - particularly the Boudicca uprising. A story so inspiring that it has been embraced tenderly down the ages, perhaps because it demonstrates solid British resolve when faced against a determined, resolute occupying force. However, if it wasn't for the Romans themselves, we would not be aware she even existed, let alone the catastrophe that occurred resulting in such a colossal loss of life. There are no written records of Boudicca, the Queen of the Iceni tribe who purportedly led her army against her Roman oppressors in a revolt so merciless it resulted in the deaths of tens of thousands of people. It is unfortunate that the native Britons of that era did not keep written records so we only have the Roman account of events that could have so nearly finished the Roman occupation of Britain back almost 2000 years ago.

We first learned of Queen Boudicca in the 16th century when manuscripts by the Roman senator and historian Publius Tacitus were discovered in Germany in 1508 by a Catholic prelate named Giovanni Angelo Arcimboldi (later an Archbishop of Milan). Arcimboldi placed the manuscripts in the Medici library in Florence and had them republished in Rome in 1515. Later British accounts of the uprising, such as Raphael Holinshed's *Chronicles of England, Scotland, and Ireland*, were first published in 1577, and Irish writer Arthur Murphy translated them again in 1794. But the legend of Boudicca didn't reach the pinnacle of popularity until the Victorian era. It was during this period that Britain was in the process of creating a sizable empire itself and looking back with pride on its ancestral roots. The notion of a strong female leader of Britain in antiquity boosted the fact that there was currently a female queen at the head of the realm who was equally as strong as her predecessor. Regrettably, as we venture into the world of multi-culturism, her popularity is in decline, and if you witness the hordes of people walking past Thomas Thornycroft's statue of *Boudicca and her Daughters* on the Thames by the houses of Parliament, barely a few afford his masterpiece a second glance.

Publius Cornelius Tacitus was a Roman historian and politician and is widely valued as one of Rome's primary historians. Tacitus was born in about 56AD, so he would only have been five or six years old when Boudicca's uprising began. His *Annals* are perhaps the closest contemporary account we have of the rebellion. He wrote about the event approximately 30 years later in his adulthood. Various scholars believe that as a young senator, Tacitus had access to *Acta Senatus,* which were written minutes and transcripts of meetings and events of the Roman Empire that were recorded and stored by the Senate. In addition, his father-in-law was Gnaeus Julius Agricola, a Roman general and senator who began his earlier career as a young Tribune serving under Paulinus during his governorship of Briton and could have quite literally been present at the battle. Tacitus could have benefitted by learning of Agricola's exploits first hand. Agricola eventually became the Governor of Britain in 78 AD.

The second source is from writer and historian: Cassius Dio, who again, was a Roman senator and historian of Greek origin. Dio was born approximately 165 AD and wrote in ancient Greek and his style is sometimes regarded as sensationalist and it has been argued that he seems to be 'piggy-backing' on what Tacitus had already chronicled years earlier - just adding some creative licence to reach the desired effect for his readers. However, Dio is recognised as a respected writer in his own right, and, as a senator also, he would have had access to *Acta Senatus* manuscripts as well. Dio published over 80 volumes of works covering the Roman Empire during his life.

That said, we must appreciate that in studying the Boudicca uprising we are examining the subject mainly through the eyes of the Roman chroniclers; thus, we must be aware that certain aspects of their accounts are subject to personal preference, sometimes favouring on misinformation for the benefit of censorship and for the entertainment of their readership. The purpose of this work however, is not to dismiss the classical writer's sequence of events entirely, but to look at the subject with an open mind trying not to be misled by certain exaggerated records of events and consider their narratives with an open mind.

The Roman historians inform us in 60-61AD Boudicca, Queen of the Iceni tribe, led an army of biblical proportions - 100,000 warriors, and possibly many more – in a revolt against Rome[i]. Her army ransacked Camulodunum (Colchester), Londinium (London) and Verulamium (St Albans), killing everyone in its path. Up to 80,000 Romans, and Britons who were loyal to Rome, are said to have been slaughtered before her vast army was stopped in its tracks by General Suetonius Paulinus and his legions, in a battle at which 80,000 Britons also perished. [ii]. The battle site has never been found.

The uprising was a tragedy for both sides: and if we are to believe the Roman historians, a total of 160,000 people were killed in the revolt, which was prompted by the apparent contempt shown to the ancient Britons by their Roman oppressors. The Romans were not unaccustomed to uprisings throughout their empire. Several other tribal leaders - such as Vercingetorix in Gaul, Spartacus in Italy, Arminius in present-day Germany, and Hannibal in Carthage in present-day Tunisia - very nearly overcame the Roman hegemony. But in Britain it is Boudicca that is remembered and revered: not just because she was a British queen, but also because she was a woman.

Neither Tacitus nor Dio offer more than tiny extracts of information about the uprising or indeed the location of the battle – known as the Battle of Watling Street – at which Paulinus's legions destroyed the revolt. Several locations along the route of Watling Street (the Roman Road that led from Dover on the south coast to Wroxeter, north of Birmingham on the River Severn, along the course of the modern day A5) have been suggested over the years. The original Watling Street was said to be 276 miles long (444kms) thus, pinpointing the battle location is challenging. The location of the battle is one of the most intriguing enigmas of British history. Many of the locations suggested have been well-researched, while others rely on unreasonable assumptions, extrapolation from local folklore, or complete invention.

Gaius Suetonius Paulinus was the Roman governor of Britain during the Boudicca uprising. Little is known of his early life, but we know he was the governor of Mauretania in 40 AD and was the first Roman commander to lead his army across the Atlas Mountains. He was transferred to Britain in approximately 58AD after the death of the existing governor: Quintus Veranius who died suddenly in office. Paulinus' policy was said to subdue the tribes of Britain aggressively which had an effect on the ultimate uprising in 61 AD.

However, the Boudicca uprising has always had a particular grip on the British imagination. Boudicca was renamed Bonduca in an early seventeenth century play of the same name, by John Fletcher, and epic poems about her were also written by Cowper and Tennyson). There are few films made about her, but that is probably due to such limited fragments of information from Roman historians, which means that feature-length films about her would inevitably contain much conjecture, and few historical facts. There have also been many TV documentaries about Boudicca in recent decades and several clips on websites, but most of them rehash old myths, and few of them break new ground. Boudicca is best remembered as a myth, not a celluloid heroine[iii].

So, we only have Roman accounts of events to go on, but it is clear that her revolt sent a shock wave that resonated all the way back to the corridors of power in Rome. Britain's Roman occupation was young, and insecure. Britain was a violent and precarious place, and it was, almost from the start, one of the most volatile parts of the empire. The Boudiccan rebellion was easily the biggest mutiny that the Romans faced in Britannia – but also the last. After the Boudiccan revolt there were no more major uprisings against the Roman colonisation of Britain, which lasted until the Romans left almost 400 years later. The failure of the revolt was thus one of the key turning points of ancient British history.

Given the colossal numbers of people killed during the uprising, it would be reasonable to believe that archaeological evidence wouldn't be too difficult to unearth. However, only two human remains have ever been found at Colchester and there are no bodies at any of the sites that can be attributed to the uprising to date. (Collingridge 206)

Archaeologists have identified evidence of fire damage that both Tacitus and Dio describe in the towns trashed by Boudicca's rebels which appears to date from the time of the revolt and confirm the Roman historians' claims that they were ransacked by British tribes.

It is difficult for historians to gather clear information, given the minuscule amount of contemporary evidence and primary sources. Two thousand years on from the Romans' arrival in Britain, much of the history of their occupation, and the battles they fought, is conjectural. Archaeological evidence is patchy, and often confusing, and, as discussed, we only have the works of Tacitus and Cassius Dio to rely on. Both wrote their accounts of the uprising many years after the event, and arguably both were the pre-curser for modern newspaper journalists informing the Roman Empire of events around the known world.

This work will argue that the battlefield has been under our noses all along, in the English home counties, just outside the town of Dunstable in Bedfordshire and approximately 12 miles from St Albans. The site is now a well-known beauty spot, visited by thousands of day-trippers each year, and right on the junction where the ancient trail: Icknield Way, crosses Watling Street. (or the ancient trail that preceded it.) The Icknield Way would have taken the Iceni all the way back to their homelands in what is today Norfolk. The question is was Paulinus and his legions waiting for them here as they made their way home from ransacking the three towns mentioned above?

[i] There are many ways of spelling Boudicca's name. Traditionally it has often been spelled Boadicea. Many modern historians refer to her as Boudica. Throughout this work I refer to her as Boudicca, with two 'c's, as a compromise.

[ii] Suetonius Paulinus is not to be confused with the historian Gaius Suetonius Tranquillus, who was not born until 68AD, six or seven years after the Boudiccan revolt. Although the general was referred to as both Suetonius and Paulinus by Roman historians, in

this work I will refer to him as Paulinus, not Suetonius, in the interests of clarity and consistency.

[iii] Intriguingly, most films about Boudicca have been made in the last 20 years. They include *Boudicca* of 2003 (released in the United States as *Warrior Queen*), *Boudicca: Rise Of The Warrior Queen* of 2019, and a new film, also called *Boudicca* and starring Olga Kurylenko, which is due to be released at the end of 2023. One of the more eccentric treatments of her story *Boudicca Bites Back* – a cine-opera made in 2008 by Ken Russell and student filmmakers from Swansea in the space of just five days. Only 16 minutes long, the film stars Russell himself, then in his early eighties, as a Roman senator.

ICENI ECEN 10-43 AD Silver unit Ecen Edn

2

The Fragile Peace

C aesar led two expeditions to Britain almost a century before the Romans finally invaded in 43 AD, He had got to know of the peoples of Britain during his wars in Gaul (which brought much of what is now France, Belgium, Luxembourg and Switzerland under Roman control between 58 and 50BC). But his two military expeditions to Britain were not intended to lead to the island's conquest. One theory is that he had hoped to stop the British mercenaries from crossing the Ocean and supporting the Gauls. (Hoffman 19) The other theory is he hoped to find gold and silver in abundance, but when he realised that the metals were only mined in minute quantities in distant regions of northern and south-western Britain, he was said to 'rapidly lose interest. (Hoffman 27-28) But he did extract 'tributes'– an agreement to provide fodder and grain to the Roman empire, in return for Caesar's promise that the empire would not invade.

Caesar gained a good understanding of southern Britain, its natural resources, and any potential value to Rome. He also came to admire the Celtic Britons' fighting skills: They were indeed a force to be regarded. And while the Roman army was technically stronger as a unit, the average Celtic Briton's physiology was said to be bigger and more muscular than the Mediterranean build of the Roman invaders. The best Legionnaires were short and stocky, with good body strength. It was of no use being a young, slim Adonis on the battlefield, you needed to be able to take on the greatest warriors. In addition, the brutality of the ancient Britons was well known to Paulinus and his legions. He knew they did not take or sell prisoners after a battle; enemy warriors were executed, and it was a common custom for Britons to decapitate their opponents and keep their heads as prizes of war. Celts believed that the decapitated head, or *tete coupée*, of a slain warrior held special powers that would be treasured always. These heads were either hung around the necks of their chariot horses to advertise their ferocity or taken back to display at their settlements.

Although they wore no body armour, British warriors looked daunting on the battlefield. They often went into battle semi-naked or sometimes completely naked, with blue woad painted onto their bodies, or tattooed permanently onto their skin[i].

Roman troops, by contrast, were very disciplined and professionalised. The Roman army had been constantly at war for hundreds of years, so knew how to respond to most situations. Its soldiers were not allowed to be married during active service, (which was often overlooked) but a career as a legionary was appealing for many Roman young men. Successful candidates would receive good pay, a pension, medical assistance, free food, accommodation, and security – and above all, Roman citizenship. A new legionnaire would have to endure a strict training regime that would make him super-fit, and battle-ready. He would be capable of marching at least 20 miles per day, carrying a full pack. At the end of each day's march, he would have to take out his trenching tools with just enough time to bivouac before nightfall. A young legionnaire might be regarded as the underdog if put against a ferocious Celtic Briton warrior one-to-one in unarmed combat, but he was technically superior, certainly strong, fit, well-trained and very intelligent.

Britain's native tribes were often at loggerheads, with conflict a regular occurrence with each other. Each tribe spoke its own language: variants of Common Brittonic, a form of ancient Celtic. The Trinovantes, a tribe living in what we now call Essex and parts of Suffolk and Hertfordshire, became friendly with the Romans during Caesar's expeditions, and made their first emergence in historical records. The Trinovantes were said to have helped Caesar in his quest to locate the stronghold of the Catuvellauni (a rival tribe to the immediate west of the Trinovantes, whose lands roughly covered Hertfordshire,

Buckinghamshire and Bedfordshire) at Wheathampstead, just north of St Albans, where the Catuvellaunian chieftain, Cassivellaunus, is said to have been defeated in battle, or surrendered. The Trinovantes' own capital was possibly in Braughing, Hertfordshire, at the time of Caesar's expeditions, but by the middle of the first century AD it seems to have moved to Colchester, much nearer the North Sea coast. Both Camulodunum (Colchester), and Verulamium (St Albans), were to pay a heavy price in Boudicca's revolt. What is somewhat confusing, is that the Catuvellauni and the Trinovantes seemed to be one under King Cunobelin from 8 – 41 AD. In addition, his coinage shows a heavy Roman influence which indicates co-operation between them all, perhaps as a 'client king' status. It is widely assumed that Cunobelin was originally king of the Catuvellauni, but other scholars challenge that view suggesting he was a Trinovantian as his first coins seemed to be minted at Colchester not St Albans. (Branigan 7) Although the Catuvallauni were bound by treaty not to attack the Trinovantes by Caesar in 54 BC, something must have occurred as both tribes were one by the third invasion of 43 AD almost a century later. Both Tactitus and Dio do not mention the Trinovantes after the revolt was put down and the Trinovantes disappear from history. (Dunnett 51)

Julius Caesar may not have been in Britain for long, and he may not have tried to conquer it properly, but he certainly learnt how the British tribes operated, and what military tactics were needed to defeat the hostile ones. The Roman conquest of Britain was gradual. Wales was not fully conquered until about 78AD, and only the southern half of Scotland was brought under Roman control in the 80s, before the Romans retreated to the Stanegate line by 87AD. (later marked by Hadrian's Wall, which was built from 122AD onwards) By 61AD only the southern two-thirds of England, south of the Humber-Mersey axis, were under Roman control, and even within this area some parts were only nominally Roman, with the rest effectively hostile areas. Mary Beard said that Britain was Rome's Afghanistan. However, the Roman conquest was to last for nearly half a millennia.

We know that the Romans had their hands full, facing attacks from marauding militias in the West Country, Wessex and most of Wales. The tribes north of the Thames did not succumb to invasion very easily either. Only south of the Thames were the Cantiaci, Regninses and Atrebates tribes completely friendly to the Romans, given their long-lasting tradition of trade with the continent, which predated the Roman occupation. In 60 AD, the Roman conquest was still in its infancy. Most Roman towns, villas and roads had yet to be built. The population of the British Isles could have been anywhere between half a million to maybe 1.5 million. But, only a fraction of these people would have been Roman, which questions the figures by the classical historians of 80,000 Romans killed during the rebellion. In total, there may have been about 100,000 Romans living in Britain, and they would have been predominately military personnel and traders. They were heavily outnumbered by the indigenous Celtic tribespeople.

The Romans practiced the taking of 'hostages' from various British tribes to Rome for a set period of time, to ensure that the tribes would behave themselves, pay the Romans 'tribute' in terms of fodder and grain, and not attack them: a practice that had started during Caesar's expeditions and resumed after the invasion in the reign of Claudius. The noun 'Hostage' is somewhat misleading though. (Oliver 343) It is not known if a hostage was ever injured or killed if Roman demands were not met, but if their tribes behaved well, they would not be badly treated. Most 'hostages' would have been close relations of tribal chieftains and nobility, and in Rome they would have been taken in by Roman families, well educated, and thoroughly Romanised. They would have been treated as citizens of Rome, and by the time they returned to their tribes their indoctrination was complete and it was anticipated that they would pass on their new culture and encourage their tribal peers to adopt the Roman way of life.

As many of the 'hostages' were from the ruling elite, it would open the way for them to develop as forthcoming rulers as the cost of full military occupation was far too excessive. This is how the Romans addressed their dilemma by introducing 'client kings' that would tow the Roman line. (Hoffman 42) However, this tactic did not always achieve success. Arminius (17/18 BC – 21 AD) was a noble prince of the Germanic tribe *Cherusci* and was taken to Rome as a child 'hostage' to be raised as Roman elite. He learnt Latin and Roman warfare and became a Roman officer. However, he eventually turned against Rome and was instrumental in causing one of Rome's heaviest defeats at the Battle of Teutoburg Forest where he led the Romans into a trap resulting in 15,000 Roman soldiers slain in 9 AD.

The Iceni tribe lived up in what is today, Suffolk and Norfolk and were protected by the dense forests, and the boggy marshland of what we now call the Fens, around their territory, and seem to have retained more autonomy than most other tribes in southern Britain. They did not seem to do any trade at all with the Romans. No amphorae or other artifacts from the continent have ever been discovered on Iceni lands that would indicate regular trading.

Tensions first arose when Publius Ostorius Scapula, the Governor of Britain from 47 to 52AD, implemented a disarmament policy in an attempt at curtailing the constant attacks on the Roman military around the whole province.

The lives of tribal Britons were hard, cruel, and often short. This way of life meant that all Britons wanted (or needed) to carry arms, whether they were warriors or not. In many tribes the noble elite took umbrage at Scapula's edict, as they saw the right to bear arms as an integral part of their cultural identity. Britain had fast become 'Rome's newest and most troublesome province' (Collingridge 129) and it was not a surprise to find an uprising springing up almost immediately in 47AD. The Iceni leader at the time: Antedios, led the revolt and was either killed or taken into slavery, he may have absconded. Either way, Scapula suppressed the revolt ruthlessly, and Antedios was never heard of again.

The Romans faced a difficult position of placing a client ruler that would tow the Roman line along with being accepted by the indigenous people. This problem was soon settled with the placement of Prasutagus as the new client king of the Iceni. Whether he was one of the 'hostages' that the Romans took is just speculation. If that was the case, then he would have been indoctrinated in the Roman way of life, able to speak Latin fluently and keep the fragile peace between both the tribal warriors and the Romans. We can only speculate about Boudicca's origins. As she was the queen of the Iceni it is likely that she had been brought up in Norfolk or Suffolk, but some have claimed that Boudicca was not Iceni at all, and that she was from the Trinovantes tribe to the south. Anyway, both Prasutagus and Boudicca being accepted candidates by the Iceni people without too much fuss, adds weight to the suggestion. Whether he returned as an adolescent and spent several years amongst the tribe before being put forward by the Romans, we can only speculate. Furthermore, we do not know if he was already married to Boudicca before he became client king or he took her as his bride when he came to the throne. However, it is said that the Iceni enjoyed 13 years of relative peace until he died in 60AD.

Prasutagus may have thought he was astute enough to know how to deal with the Romans effectively during his reign and we believe there was no Roman military presence of Iceni lands until after his death.(Wood 20) But all that was to change. Dio claims that a dispute with the Romans over money soon escalated into a bitter quarrel that resulted in the threatening of the Iceni's cultural pride, and their very right to exist. Much trouble lay ahead.

Dio claims that Prasutagus received considerable loans from Claudius which he used to help the Iceni people were not being repaid. Apparently, Claudius held Prasutagus in high regard and had been lenient about repayment terms. But after Claudius died in 54AD the incoming emperor - Claudius's adopted son, Nero - was not so accommodating. Prasutagus was said to try and satisfy the new emperor with gifts and goods, but he was virtually ignored by his administration. The Romans now wanted their money back.

Decianus, Britain's Roman procurator (in effect its financial chief), demanded repayment in full. The bailiffs had come calling, and they had the full backing of Rome. Dio claims that the Romans were now becoming impatient, and soon after Prasutagus's death, matters came to a head. What is confusing is why Prasutagus would have taken out loans in the first place. They did not seem to adopt the Roman way of life at all. There is no evidence of trade between them; there were no buildings of any description that would constitute needing considerable loans to enable construction. Indeed, the Iceni did not seem to have a major town like the Trinovantes who had Camulodunum

– (Colchester), or the Catuvellauni who had Verulamium – (St Albans) We know there were small Iceni settlements in Thetford and Caister St Edmond – just south of Norwich, but no major place that could be called a town.

It is arguable that there had been any loan at all.– It could be argued that both Tacitus and Dio may have intentionally misled their Roman readers to justify the brutality of the Roman actions with regard to the Iceni lands for the sake of their readership.

To make the situation worse, Prasutagus was said to have left his estate to be shared equally between his two daughters – who have never been identified by name - and the Roman emperor himself: Nero. As we know the ancient Britons were not adept at writing things down and recording events, thus the issue of how Prasutagus left his will is challenging. If it was a written document that was sent to Nero, we will never know. However, if there ever was a written document, it lends credibility to the theory that he had learned to read and write Latin in Rome.

What is known is that the Romans were not satisfied by the bequest of half of Prasutagus's estate. Suetonius, writing in the second century AD, claimed that Nero "even considered withdrawing from Britain, and only refrained from doing so out of deference – so that he should not appear to be belittling his father's glory". If this was ever true, Nero's desire to quit Britain had evaporated by the early 60s. Instead, Nero now wanted to tighten his grip.

Why Prasutagus did not include his wife Boudicca in his will is unclear. Perhaps he feared that if she inherited his kingdom the Romans would have been enraged, and that passing half of his estate to his daughters and the other half to Nero was a safer option to keep the fragile peace. Some scholars have suggested that the Romans would not take likely to a female queen, but there had been Queen Cartimandua of the Brigantes up in what is today Yorkshire, who ruled from around 43 AD to 69 AD.

Boudicca may have come from another tribe, through an arranged marriage, and leaving the bulk of his estate to a 'foreigner' may have rattled the Iceni elite and led to a power struggle. However,

Prasutagus's death lit the fuse of the Iceni's revolt regardless. The Romans annexed the Iceni's territory, ending their relative autonomy, and helped themselves to all that it had to offer. The booty-hungry Romans seem to have shown complete contempt towards the Iceni people. As Tacitus wrote:

> *'His kingdom was looted by centurions, his house by slaves, as if they were the bounty of war. All the chief men of the Iceni, as if Rome had received the whole country as a gift, were stripped of their ancestral estates, and the king's relatives were made slaves (Tacitus XIV 31)*

Prasutagus' decision to sidestep his wife in favour of his daughters and Emperor Nero did not curtail the Roman land grab. Even more humiliatingly, Boudicca is said to have been publicly flogged by the Romans. Boudicca herself was not apparently raped, but her two daughters were, and it is easy to understand how the Iceni people, who were proud of their relative independence from the Roman yoke, would have been outraged by these humiliations, and the Romans seem to have under-estimated the native Britons' resolve, and the dangers posed by the hornets' nest that they had just disturbed. They were about to experience the wrath of British tribes as never before.

Thrill seekers over the defile

3

The Rebellion

Tensions were also rising further south, in the lands of the Trinovantes in modern Essex. Although the Trinovantes had accepted the Romans into their territory during Caesar's expeditions, they had done so primarily because the Romans offered them protection from the neighbouring Catuvellauni tribe. But more than a century later, the Trinovantes had little to thank the Romans for. Soon after the Roman invasion in 43AD the Romans had designated Camulodnum (Colchester), in the north of the Trinovantes' lands, as the new capital of Roman Britannia. In addition, the construction of the Temple of Claudius, the immense temple built in the honour of the Emperor, stood prominently in the centre of town. However, the locals resented it vehemently, and looked beyond its grandeur and saw it as a metaphor for Roman oppression.

In 49AD the XX Legion (20th) moved from Colchester to Glevan in modern-day Gloucester and then in AD 57, it moved again to Usk in South Wales. which left Colchester relatively undefended. At the same time, Veteran Roman legionnaires who had finished their military service were rewarded with gifts of productive farmland in and around Colchester by Scapula. A shortage of trained troops with an emperor unwilling to send any more left him with a dilemma. Instead of retiring them off and sending them home, Scapula offered the veterans large tracts of quality land around the *colonia* as a pension to keep them in the –province. These farmsteads would have provided a good lifestyle for the veterans and Scapula had access to a sort of 'dads army' that could be called on in the event on an emergency. (Hunt 49) By 60 AD the arrogance of these veterans however, and the increasing numbers of settlers on Trinovantes' territory, meant that the Trinovantes became just as resentful of the Romans as the Iceni were.

There is some doubt about the month, or even the year that Boudicca's uprising occurred. Perhaps it began in the early summer of 61AD – possibly in May. Like others, Webster believes that the uprising took place in 60AD, but Waite states that it took place during the consulships of Lucius Caesennius Paetus and Publius Petronius Turpilianus – which was 61 AD. (Waite p64) We are told that the Trinovantes did not sow their fields that spring, and both Tacitus and Dio inform us it was in protest against the Roman legions taking the lion's share of their harvests. Though, it is unlikely the tribes would have put themselves and their livestock at that much risk of shortages. Tacitus and Dio may have chronicled this for the benefit of their readership by creating a mental picture of impending doom. In reality, it is conceivable that the real reason could have been due to a poor harvest the previous year so they left the majority of their fields fallow that year. Furthermore, Einkorn has been found in the burnt ashes in London indicating that grain was still being brought in from the continent for Roman consumption.

As the military had left to advance on Wales, Colchester only had a small contingent of soldiers remaining in the town and was arguably left exposed without adequate defences in the event of a crisis. Therefore, it is debatable that the town's residents began to wear arms again to counter the lack of security and perhaps a show of solidarity between the local townsfolk against the ever-growing settlers. This may have alarmed the remaining Roman citizens who suspected trouble brewing resulting in them sending a plea to Decianus for assistance.

It could be argued that there was not a sudden or spontaneous assault on Colchester, but a gradual increase in tensions as the population began to swell. The Iceni were edging southwards and would soon meet with the restive Trinovantes in the town. There is evidence that the Iceni attacked other targets on their way to Colchester. Remnants of a burned Roman villa have been found between the villages of Foxton and Shepreth in Cambridgeshire, where the remains of a man and a woman (probably the building's occupants) were discovered. Evidence of human Skeletons have also been found by the river Rhee nearby, which suggests that there may have been a skirmish here, while they were enroute from Norfolk. If the rebels had encroached on Colchester *enmasse* and without warning, its residents would not have had time to send a messenger to Decianus asking for help. A slow and sustained influx of armed Britons over several days makes more sense.

The Romans were said to be very superstitious and just prior to the troubles, Cassius Dio claims, the town experienced terrifying portents of trouble ahead: a statue of Victory suddenly fell over, and a theatre was filled with the sound of ominous shrieks. Nearer London, the waters of the Thames estuary turned blood-red, and in them Romans saw images of their impending overthrow. Perhaps another example of Dio's creativity in capturing the attention of his readers.

In response, procurator Decianus sent 200 troops from London to reinforce the Romans' miniscule garrison there to deter trouble. But the 200 legionaries were far too few. It may have taken several days from the request for reinforcements to their arrival in Colchester: two days for a message to reach London, three days for the troops to be mustered, and three days for them to reach Colchester on foot. They were poorly equipped, and they arrived too late to stop a violent uprising. Indeed, the arrival of the 200 troops may have not helped in keeping the townsfolk calm and may have been the spark that set the revolt off.

It appears that a further plea for urgent reinforcements was sent to Petillius Cerialis, commander of the IX Hispana legion (9th) at Longthorpe (on the edge of Peterborough, where the Thorpe Wood golf course now stands, and a good 70 miles north-east of Colchester). But the IX legion never arrived, and the small Roman military presence in Colchester was powerless to stop the town being razed, and many of its Roman citizens slaughtered. Army veterans and their families are said to have sought safety in the grand temple, but after a two-day siege it was taken by storm, and we believe that all of its occupants were slain.

It would have taken a forced march of at least four days for the IX legion to reach Colchester from Longthorpe. Roman soldiers could march 25 Roman miles per day under extreme circumstances, but this fast pace would have been detrimental to troops and meant that they were less battle-ready when they arrived in Colchester. To maintain their morale and fitness, troops need hearty meals, dry clothes and comfortable rest every night. If there were no marching camps enroute, troops would have had to make camp in hostile areas before nightfall, dig defensive ditches, cut sharpened stakes, and take rotas on sentry duty. Dismantling these makeshift camps was just as important as setting them up. Early each morning, the legionaries would have to pack up and set fire to the camp, to erase any sign that they had been there and to avoid leaving a camp that could be of use to hostile forces. Even the fittest Roman troops would have felt the strain after a few days. The unrelenting toil would have exhausted them, and they would have been useless in a sustained battle.

So, it is easy to understand how the IX legion could have been easily overcome in a surprise attack by Iceni forces. Like many other events of the Boudiccan uprising, the location of the massacre is not known. Aldhouse-Greene suggests that the attack happened DURING the assault on the town. (Hoffman 101) Some historians assume that it took place enroute to Colchester, as the IX legion neared its destination, though the historian Richard Hunt has claimed that it occurred much nearer Longthorpe (Hunt 85) soon after the Romans headed off from there. It is also unclear how they were ambushed, but quite possibly the result of a guerrilla assault. What is known is that about 2,000 legionaries – possibly 40% of the legion's strength of 5,000 – were slaughtered. Only the legion's cavalry managed to escape. Petillius Cerialis survived, and he had to take his remaining troops back to the safety of their fort in Longthorpe.

Thus Camulodunum (Colchester), was then the first town to receive the wrath of the ancient Britons. Although not the oldest town in England, (Amesbury claims to be a settlement since approx. 9000 BC, but there are several other contenders) Colchester though, is the oldest recorded town. There has been human settlement there dating back to the Neolithic, but after the conquest in 43 AD, the town was established and it remained the provincial capital in the first century AD.

Dio describes how Boudicca's army looted and burned everything in their path. Dio's account contains harrowing details of British atrocities against Roman citizens who had suffered at their hands. "The most atrocious and bestial committed was this," wrote Dio. "They hung up naked the noblest and most beautiful women, cut off their breasts and sewed them to their mouths so that they seemed to be eating them. Then they impaled them on sharp stakes which ran the length of their bodies". Some scholars suggest that this occurred in London, but that is debatable as London was said to have been mostly evacuated before Boudicca's forces arrived and it is unlikely that the Roman citizens would have remained to welcome the rebel force.

But this sort of atrocity was no worse than what the Romans might do when they defeated a hostile army or captured an enemy city. 'You can often see not only the bodies of human beings but also dogs sliced in two and the dismembered limbs of other animals'. (Bédoyére 209) Although the Romans looked down on the Britons as barbarians, they had few qualms about slaughtering every living thing themselves. Tacitus once wrote "Once the killing had started, it was difficult to stop", Indeed, they even spent their social time watching extreme bloodshed either by witnessing gladiators cutting each other to pieces or watching executions for their enjoyment.

Boudicca, meanwhile, seems to have become an inspiring orator as well as a military leader. Dio's account of her uprising includes the long text of a speech that she gave to her forces, spear in hand, just before an early battle: possibly the assault on Colchester. As well as appealing to national pride and attacking the greed of the occupiers, she taunted the Romans, who had "encased themselves in helmets breastplates and greaves, and have built themselves stockades, walls and trenches so as not to suffer any harm from enemy attack." Unlike the British, Boudicca argued, the Romans couldn't go to ground in swamps and mountains, and they were "incapable of enduring hunger and thirst, cold or heat as we do". "Let us show them that they are hares and foxes attempting to rule over dogs and wolves", she concluded. Dio claims that Boudicca then released a hare, which ran off on the "lucky side" as a good omen of victory", and she then mocked emperor Nero: "though he has the title of a man, he is in fact a woman, as his singing and playing the lyre and painted face declare".

Queen Boudicca is still seen as a local heroine in Colchester: there is a modern statue of her in the town, five metres high outside a well-known supermarket, and a Boadicea Bar & Restaurant. It was the largest town in England, and the *de facto* capital of Roman Britain. If Boudicca was looking for a symbol of Roman domination to attack, not far south of the Iceni's territory, Colchester was the obvious choice. Its Roman walls (parts of which still stand today) were only built between 65 and 80AD, in the wake of Boudicca's uprising. This construction was akin to closing the stable door long after the horse had bolted.

The Race to London

After the torture, killings and festivities had finished at Camulodunum (Colchester), it was time to move on to the next destination. Paulinus and his senior staff fully expected the rebels to head straight for Verulamium (St Albans) – the second *colonia* - but they headed south to Londinium instead. But why did they choose Londinium over Verulamium? Both settlements are roughly the same distance from Camulodunum (Colchester), – approximately 70 miles by today's roads. Maybe they were in search of supplies, but were Boudicca and her Iceni tribe even aware of the existence of Londinium? The Trinovantes would have been aware of its being, and perhaps knew of its grain stores, but the Iceni, hidden up behind the dense forests and Fens of what is now Norfolk might not have even heard of it. Another theory is that they could have just been pursuing the remnants of the Roman population of Camulodunum (Colchester), who managed to flee along the trail that led to Londinium in their lust for more Roman blood.

Londinium was becoming an important trading port. It had large stores of grain along with other essential commodities such as salt and iron, which were brought in from the continent. If these stores fell into the Briton's hands, it would be a disaster for Paulinus as the Britons would have a better chance of ridding themselves of their invaders for good. The Roman army relied heavily on grain, and it was normal practice to keep a year's supply of it at each military fort and grain store. (Brewer 16). The Britons could survive the summer quite easily by going back to a hunter-gatherer existence for their own sustenance and use the grain supplies seized from London granary stores for their livestock. Their main problem was that there were now far too many of them.

Londinium was not yet a large Roman town so had a small military presence and had only been established in the late 40s AD. In 61AD it was not classified as a Roman colony or a municipium (as Verulamium had been since 50AD), But while it was small, London was strategically important, as the easternmost place where the river Thames could be crossed by a dedicated crossing. There was only one crossing over the Thames in London in those days – near to where London Bridge is today, and even then, it was probably a pontoon ferry as the Thames at this point is approximately 300 metres wide. (1000 feet) and the waters are tidal with strong currents. Although archaeologists discovered evidence of a wooden 'bridge' a hundred metres or so downstream of the landmark, it is unlikely that it would have spanned the whole river. It could be argued that it is probably the remains of a jetty that reached out into the tidal reaches to enable the trading ships to remain in deep water whilst docking at London. In addition, a low-level bridge spanning the entire river would have effectively cut off settlements upstream such as Putney and Brentford to sail ships, and it is beyond the sphere of fantasy to suggest that there was a magnificently engineered masterpiece constructed high enough to allow sail ships to pass underneath in 61 AD.

If indeed, Boudicca and her senior leaders were aware of the importance of Londinium, then they would be eager to help themselves to the grain stores before going south to create havoc amongst the pro-Roman tribes of the southeast. Boudicca would be able to destroy almost everything in her path with such a large army at her disposal without too much resistance and could even get as far as the coastal settlements without too much trouble. Paulinus needed to act fast to prevent her from doing so at all costs to stop a catastrophe, so destroying the crossing at Londinium was crucial.

Both Dio and Tacitus say that the Romans did indeed reach Londinium before Boudicca. This is where the time scales of the Roman response time estimated by the plethora of scholars becomes problematic. At the time that Boudicca's forces attacked Colchester, Paulinus' forces were said to be just off the coast of Wales, on Mona (Anglesey), slaughtering the Druids. Paulinus was effectively the joint head of Roman Britannia, working alongside its civilian procurator: Catus Decianus. But as soon as the Boudiccan rebellion began, Decianus is said to have fled from London to Gaul, which left Paulinus at the helm alone and in Anglesey, some 250 miles away from where they needed to be to bring the situation under control.

In 60-61 AD, Wales was still a very dangerous place to be. It was full of hostile tribes namely the Silures, Demetae, Ordovices and Decangli, and the Romans were still far from bringing them into check. In addition, on the island of Mona (Anglesey) - across the body of water called the Menai Strait was the spiritual stronghold of the Druids.

Paulinus was said to be trying to exterminate them as they held a great amount of influence and power over the tribes of ancient Britain. If he could bring them to heel, the tribes might just yield. Indeed, Professor Jean Markale stated that Rome regarded the Druids as *'an absolute threat to the Roman State because their science and philosophy contradicted Roman orthodoxy'. (Collingridge 160)*

Tacitus claims that Paulinus himself got to London before it fell to the Britons. "For his part Suetonius [Paulinus] made his way undaunted through the mist of the enemy to London". However, it is unlikely he would have made the 'gamblers dash' to London with only a small cavalry escort. (Fuentes 312) Paulinus was far too important to risk travelling through hostile country all the way to London, and that he "decided to sacrifice a single town in order to save the whole province" and refused to stay and defend it. "Neither the tears nor the lamentations of those who begged his help could deflect him from giving the signal to pull out and allowing into his column [only] those who could keep up with him",

In reality, Paulinus would have needed to stay with the bulk of his army, rather than go on risky expeditions into enemy territory. Instead of going to London himself, his entire army that was available to him may well have established a base somewhere near St Albans, possibly along the river Ver, which in those days, was a much larger river than it is today. He would then have sent a small cavalry party of junior officers and men from there to London to reconnoitre the area.

It would have been rational for the Roman contingent who entered Londinium to send the remaining citizens of the settlement across the river to the safer southern side to seek refuge with the more pro-Roman tribes. Some of the wealthier merchants may have boarded ships to the continent, as Decianus did, and perhaps took a proportion of their belongings with them. But it would have been very unwise of the Roman commanders to take the remaining townsfolk with them back up along the trail called Watling Street as many scholars surmise. Indeed, experienced Roman commanders were very reluctant to take on civilians who would hamper their advance and drain their supplies. (Hunt 101) Furthermore, most civilians would have struggled to keep up with the group. Thus, it is more than probable that the occupants were sent across the river before they destroyed the crossing. Furthermore, the granaries were burnt on both sides of the river as quickly as possible as Boudicca and her rebels could have been moments away from the town's walls.

It is unlikely that Boudicca and her forces even knew that Paulinus was trying to prevent them from crossing the river. It could be argued that they were just running amok with not much of a battle plan whatsoever, just scouring the countryside in search of Roman blood and food. However, the river at London would not provide drinking water for their substantial needs as it is tidal. Boudicca and her leaders now faced a dilemma.

It would have taken several days for such a large army column, several miles long to cross the river. But did they actually want to cross? The Iceni were now over a hundred miles from their homelands and crossing the river would perhaps be a bridge too far. Some of the leaders were now voicing their concerns as their supplies would now be critically low, which could have been a reason a breakaway group headed west along the north-bank of the river.

Indeed, it is worth considering that the rebels surmised that the Romans themselves would cross the river to the more pro-Roman tribes along the south coastal regions to regroup and replenish the army. Militarily, that would make sense, but it is unlikely that Boudicca would have been aware of Paulinus' dilemma. If Boudicca could get to London before them, she could effectively cut them off from the south and destroy them using guerrilla tactics with her overwhelming numbers. But the small expeditionary force that reached London first did not cross the river as she would have expected. They stayed and waited for their arrival, and as soon as the rebels entered Londinium, they encountered an empty settlement with no supplies and no way of crossing the water. As soon as the fighters spotted each other, the Roman cavalry unit turned tail and headed out of the township on the trail that led to Verulamium, enticing the rebel forces in pursuit.

Paulinus did not abandon London to its fate; it was effectively evacuated and made safe. He was now enticing the huge rebel army to pursue them back to Verulamium and onto the chosen battle site just northwest of the *colonia*.

The Road to Verulamium

The Roman unit knew that to survive, they would need to stay one step ahead of the rebels at a pace that they could not catch up with them. The main procession would have been travelling at a snail's pace but many of the younger elites would have been at the vanguard of the column. Should the younger warrior elites indeed manage to apprehend the Roman column, it would have resulted in internecine confrontations that would have resulted in heavy casualties on both sides, but it is more than probable that the rebels with their superior numbers would have prevailed eventually using hit-and-run tactics.

It was well known of the vulnerability of an army on the march. Indeed, there were many dangers during journeys through hostile country and it was very difficult to fend off ambushes which would have resulted in chaos along the lines. In the unlikely event that there were civilians tagging along as well, they would be helpless and again would have experienced a gruesome demise like the occupants of Colchester. With all the townsfolk safely across the river to the south bank, the Romans only had to the worry of keeping the rebels at bay until they reached their chosen battle ground.

Boudica's path out of Londinium is widely accepted to have been northwest towards Verulamium (St Albans) where there is archaeological evidence of damage dating to the revolt. However, the extent of the damage found at St Albans is not equivalent to that of Colchester. In addition, there is also evidence of damage along the north bank of the River Thames at Putney, Brentford, and Staines. (Hoffman p102-3) In 2010 archaeologists claimed that there is evidence that Silchester (Calleva) itself was burned at some point between 60 and 80AD, which may have indeed been attacked by some British forces[iii].

Did some of the rebels break away at Londinium? - But what tribe headed west, and how many? The decision to break away could have been due to tribal clashes or disputes by ethnic leaders; it could also be that there were not enough supplies and water, so a faction decided that it might be easier to find provisions along the riverbank than heading northwest towards St Albans. Perhaps they headed upstream to see if they could locate another crossing for their wagons.

But the evidence of destruction in Silchester (Calleva) is even much less than in St Albans, and Calleva is not mentioned in either Tacitus or Cassius Dio's accounts of the Boudiccan uprising. So, we must assume that most, if not all, of Boudicca's forces ended up in St Albans, and after that there is no written record of any other towns being burned by them, just small evidence of damage outside of the *colonia.* If Paulinus had set up camp somewhere north of London after heading down from north Wales, as seems likely, his forces and the British ones were now in close proximity. It was only a matter of time before they met face-to-face in battle.

After London was burned – possibly in May 61 – it may have taken at least another 6-10 days for the Britons to reach Verulamium. (St Albans) and by now, their supplies would have been critically low. As the crow-flies, St Albans is approx. 19 miles, but with winding trails it could have been double that. The Britons may have possibly reached the *colonia* in June.

Verulamium, (St Albans) sits on the banks of the river Ver, a natural filtered chalk stream just 28kms (17Miles) long. Its source is at the foothills of the Chilterns and rises just outside Dunstable and meanders through Redbourn and Verulamium, finally flowing into the river Colne at Bricket Wood approximately 5 miles south of the city. It was an early iron-age settlement which was originally called Gwerllam meaning 'dwelling by the water' by the Casii or Catuvellauni tribe. The river's waters were crystal clear after being naturally filtered through the underlying chalk substrate which made it an ideal place for a settlement with a plentiful supply of clean, fresh water. This historic city has experienced its fair share of goings-on throughout history. Two battles during the Wars of the Roses and it was the birthplace of Britain's first saint – St Albans,

As it was a Catuvellauni town, whose inhabitants were said to be much friendlier to the Romans than the Iceni and the Trinovantes were. Verulamium's residents had been assimilated with Rome, and Webster describes it as a "Romanised City for the Britons".

But when the Britons arrived in Verulamium, they too found it largely empty. The town had been evacuated by the locals who were probably pre-warned of the uprising and had been anticipating their arrival. Its houses had even been emptied of furniture and archaeological evidence suggests that not the entire town was burned by the rebels. The extent of the damage was less than what has been found in Colchester and Waite suggested that the Britons' goal in St Albans was not simply to destroy the town and kill any inhabitants they found, but to steal as much food and equipment as they could. This is an interesting point, as this indicates the Romans did indeed destroy the grain stores before they left London and prevented the rebels from raiding the granaries there. If this is the case, then with such huge numbers they could not sustain themselves as they did not have proper and systematic supply lines to feed such a large army column, which could have forced the splinter group to break away in London. Therefore, it is probable that Boudicca now needed supplies urgently.

Yet Dio suggests that it was Paulinus who was running out of supplies and that he was forced to engage the rebel forces earlier than he might have liked to. "Fear of the natives' numbers and their mad fury dissuaded him from risking everything against them," - "Rather, he was inclined to put off the battle till a more suitable occasion, but since he was short of food and there was no let-up in the native onslaught, he was forced to engage them, even against his better judgment". This implies that Paulinus suddenly changed his plans, and rather than wait until the ideal time to meet the Britons at his selected battle site, he decided to bring them to the sword soon after the fall of St Albans. This is unlikely, Paulinus would have needed to stick to his battle plan and draw the rebels to the selected site as planned. He just needed to get the rebels there urgently. However, it could be argued that if the Romans did destroy the supply stores of London, there is a chance that their supplies were seriously disrupted also.

Historians suggest that Boudicca and her rebels then made their way out of Verulamium up Watling Street towards the midlands - Possibly still pursuing the small Roman cavalry unit in a north-westerly direction towards the crossing with the Icknield Way at

Dunstable. Between Verulamium and High Cross, five Roman towns were built on Watling Street: Dunstable (Durocobrivis). Magiovinium (Dropshort, on the eastern fringes of modern Milton Keynes), Lactodurum (Towcester, Northants) Bannaventa (Whilton Lodge, Northants) and Tripontium (Caves Inn, Warwickshire). But many of these places would not have been established by 61AD, and if they had they would have been merely settlements, not towns. And there is no evidence of burning or other destruction at any of these communities. The last of any evidence of damage is to a homestead approximately two kilometres north-west of *Verulamium* and after that the archaeological trail ceases. With no evidence of any other damage up the trail called Watling Street, it is very unlikely that Boudicca ever travelled as far north as High Cross or Mancetter, and even more unlikely that she travelled as far as Wales.

Tacitus, meanwhile, wrote that "By now Suetonius [Paulinus] had the XIV legion together with detachments from the XX and auxiliaries from the nearest stations, in all about 10,000 armed men, and at this point he resolved to abandon delay and fight". As this passage comes immediately after an account of the plunder of St Albans, it suggests that the battle took place not long after St Albans fell, and not far away from the town, so it is more than probable that Paulinus and his legions were already in the vicinity of St Albans as suspected. Boudicca may have needed supplies even more urgently. These are all strong arguments against the battle occurring in the Midlands as neither army would have had enough resources to march there.

So far, the revolt had all gone Boudicca's way. Three towns had been easily captured and effectively destroyed, half a Roman legion had been slaughtered, and what was left of the Roman army in Britain seemed to be on the run. Tacitus implies that the Roman occupation of Britain 'hung in the balance'. "A legion that had ventured battle had been destroyed; the rest were skulking in their camps or looking for a chance of escape. They would not withstand even the din and clamour of so many warriors, still less their onslaught and blows". With typical hyperbole, Cassius Dio would later write that "the island [of Britain] fell into the hands of the enemy".

What Boudicca and her rebels did not know is that they were being lured to the chosen battle site. All Paulinus needed to do now was get them to follow his small unit out of *Verulamium* towards the Dunstable Downs where the chosen battle site was located. The Romans were not in fact preparing to flee Britain. Instead, they were preparing for a final reckoning, which would soon come close to wiping out her entire army.

[i] Cassius Dio claimed that the immediate cause of the rebellion was not the humiliation of Boudicca and her daughters, but money: the loan of 10 million drachmas (40 million sesterces) that Seneca (a philosopher and statesman who was a close adviser of emperor Nero at the time of the Boudiccan revolt) had made to the British tribal leaders in Claudius's day, and which was now demanded back; "all at once and in a heavy-handed manner". Only now does Boudicca enter Dio's account, as "the one person thought worthy of leading them", and "a woman of the Royal family who possessed more spirit than is usual among women". It is arguable that there had been any loan: why did the Iceni need the money? They had their own currency and their own way of life, and they did not like to drink Roman wine: no amphorae have ever been found in Iceni lands. Dio may have intentionally misled his Roman readers to justify the brutality of the Roman response to Boudicca's uprising.

[ii] See http://news.bbc.co.uk/local/ berkshire/hi/people _and_places/history/newsid_ 8646000/8646066.stm.

'Boudicca'
Character Sketches of Romance, Fiction and the Drama
Ebenezer Cobham Brewer (p270, 1892)
Internet Archive Book Images

4

Preparing For Battle

Research indicates that the battle site was at a location of the Roman's choosing. Indeed, Paulinus could not possibly offer battle unless it was on his terms. The Britons were well known as fierce fighters, and would fight anywhere, and being against such a ferocious adversary with such overwhelming numbers, the Romans would need to choose the battle ground carefully to have any chance of surviving this conflict.

Paulinus needed to assemble his forces urgently, and in doing so he would have learned of the dilemma he now faced. Sending his messengers to both the IX Hispania in Longthorpe near today's Peterborough and II Augusta at Exeter requesting their immediate assistance would soon make him aware that the situation was a lot more serious than he thought. Estimating that Paulinus was near Verulamium (St Albans) at the time, his orders to the other two legions would have been to rendezvous with the main army as quickly as possible, quite possibly at the selected battle site at Dunstable - at the crossroads of Icknield Way and Watling Street.

In theory the four legions under his command in Britain had a combined strength of about 20,000 (about 5,000 troops in each legion), plus roughly the same number of auxiliary troops, Gaullish mercenaries (drawn from present-day France and Belgium), plus some captured Britons who were forced to fight for the Roman side in return for their lives. This would have meant a total force of about 40,000. But 2,000 of these men had just been slaughtered, and most of the rest were scattered far and wide.

The II Augusta legion was stationed in Isca Dumnoniorum (Exeter) approximately 200 miles southwest of Colchester where they built a fort there. They could get back to the battle site heading back towards Verulamium using the existing ancient trails: Wessex Ridgeway, Ridgeway and then Icknield Way at Ivinghoe and continue the short distance to Pascombe Pit on Dunstable Downs. But they never arrived to help quell the Boudiccan revolt. In addition, the annihilation of the foot soldiers from the IX legion had effectively been put out of action leaving Paulinus with just two legions remaining: the XIV Gemina and the XX Valeria – and we are led to believe, were hundreds of miles away from the trouble spots. Before him faced an army of significant numbers and he was without two of the four legions under his control.

Paulinus's military expedition to Wales would have been a risky undertaking requiring complicated logistics. Like Caesar a century earlier, Paulinus would have had to take elaborate steps to keep his supply lines open. We are aware that it is said that 500 pack animals were required for each legion, to haul tents, clothing, cooking equipment, armour, spare weapons, food, fodder and medical equipment: everything that is needed to keep an efficient army on the move. Because of the need to maintain base camps, he had probably left many of his troops along his route in and out of north Wales as keeping clear supply lines is crucial in any military operation. The XIV was a full Legion, but the XX was not. Webster has speculated that Paulinus may have had only seven or eight thousand legionaries, plus between four and five thousand auxiliaries: a force of between 12 or 13,000 troops at the most. But as an experienced commander-in-chief he would not have taken all these men to Anglesey. Many of them would be elsewhere along the trails guarding the marching camps and keeping the supply routes open. He would have needed to keep his escape routes clear.

Even if Paulinus had got word of the Boudiccan rebellion from his array of messengers, within a few days of it starting he couldn't have marched immediately south-eastwards from Mona (Anglesey) at full speed. Paulinus would have been slowed down by logistical problems: Fear of ambushes, and the need to dismantle the string of temporary marching camps he had set up enroute; and to pick up their equipment and personnel along the way. In addition, he would have been further impeded by the walking wounded - casualties accrued during the many skirmishes during the campaign. He would not have been able to leave them behind. A forced march of 250 miles is not realistic, even the horses and pack animals could not sustain that.

Napoleon Bonaparte notably said that an army marches on its stomach in the aftermath of his disastrous invasion of Russia in 1812. The harsh winters that Russia endures added to the huge losses of his Grande Armée of over 400,000 soldiers. On their retreat less than 20,000 men came back, struggling to cross the frozen Berezina River in modern Belarus with the Russians in hot pursuit. The poor road conditions did not assist Napoleon's advance on Moscow making the movement of their baggage trains challenging. With the roads being in such a poor state of repair, the large baggage trains would have turned them into impassable quagmires within a short period of time. The outnumbered Russian's initial refusal to engage in battle and subsequent withdrawal back to Moscow expanded Napoleon's dilemma. Furthermore, their scorched-earth policy, by decimating everything in their path as they withdrew to Moscow ensured that Napoleon could not obtain any supplies off the land whatsoever as he advanced towards them.

Yet centuries prior to Napoleon, the Roman commanders knew of the importance of keeping and maintaining supply lines for their troops. It is well documented that the Romans were experienced in providing for their armies. They also knew the importance of constructing robust roads to allow for the rapid movements of both troops and supplies which enabled them to increase the size of the empire and push further inland through areas such as Spain, Greece, Asia Minor and North Africa with relative ease.

Julius Caesar landed in Britain with 5 legions, support cavalry and support auxiliaries, totalling a force of approximately 30,000 personnel during his second invasion in 54 BC. To ensure security and to maintain supplies he left one legion at his beachhead on the coast of Kent before encroaching inland with his remaining forces. He then left a large contingent of troops at each marching camp along his course before he forded the Thames at East Tilbury, finally sacking

Wheathampstead - the stronghold of the Catuvellani with just 2 legions remaining. (Nolan 100)

Without proper nourishment, soldiers would be of little use to an ambitious commander like Caesar. Indeed, the Roman military manuals stressed the need for soldiers to eat before fighting. A weak army would soon be overwhelmed without too much effort by a well-fed adversary. The Romans were expert foragers, (so were the ancient Britons) and every Roman soldier carried a sickle to enable fodder to be gathered for the livestock. They would grab whatever food they could in the summer months, and stock up for the winter. The vast forests of Britain had plenty of berries, deer, fruit, fungi, game birds, hare, lynx, rabbit, waterfowl and wild boar. Rivers and streams provided plenty of clean water, and fish.

Foraging in enemy territory was always essential, but also very dangerous. Should legionnaires venture too far away from their group they were open to attack by roaming militia. Plus moving these foodstuffs to the right place, in the right quantities, was always a logistical challenge. Aside from Caesar's human forces, he also had many horses, oxen, and other pack animals, which required much fodder and grain. But fodder does not grow in abundance in dense woodland. Boudicca's army would equally have consisted of tens of thousands of people, stretching over quite a considerable distance complete with wagons, animals, women and children walking at a snail's pace along the trails.

Paulinus would have known it was safer for the main army to stay together than split into several groups. Thus, the notion of him breaking away to London is not credible. It would have been foolish for the general and commander of two legions to travel through hostile territory with a small cavalry contingent as they would be open to attack almost all the way back until he reached the safety of the Catuvellauni territory of St Albans. You need large numbers when travelling through hostile country (Nolan 100) Although Paulinus may not have heard the fate of the IX Legion at this stage, he certainly would have known that his forces were very vulnerable when on the march. The loss of Paulinus himself in an ambush enroute would have had a disastrous effect on morale among the Roman ranks, and on the future of the Roman occupation. The Romans could not fight guerrilla wars effectively, so accordingly there has to be another explanation. Furthermore, Watling Street was certainly not built that far into hostile territory by 61AD. If Watling Street existed at all, it would have only been south of the Thames where the tribes were pro-Roman and even then, it would have still been under construction.

The Roman occupation of Britain was only in its seventeenth or eighteenth year. The Romans were kept busy fighting hostile tribes, building forts and marching camps, and establishing towns. Paving roads with stone required roadbuilding teams, which required peace. If hostile Celt tribes were still at large, attacking Romans at will, then roadbuilding would have required military protection, which would have been very burdensome. It would have taken decades, if not centuries, for Britain's' network of Roman roads to be fully cobbled. Hoffman, does not believe that Wating Street was paved until about 150 AD, and Webster says it may not have been paved until 250 AD, or even later. Although there may have been a Celtic track following the same course that Watling Street was later built on, it would have mostly gone through dense woodland, where the ground never fully dries out even in summer. As the track would have been unpaved, it would have been quickly reduced to a muddy quagmire by a large army marching in line. The existing trails of Britain were only designed for small hunter - gatherer parties that would not have left too much impact on the environment, large army columns would.

Assuming that all the forces Paulinus had with him in Wales were still with him, he would have had probably no more than 12,000 or 13,000 men. The British however, had 100,000 and anything up to 230,000, if Cassius Dio is to be believed. He was greatly outnumbered. The Romans' best chance of victory lay in using fortifications, and the lay of the land. Paulinus could not allow his smaller army to be surrounded or they would be overwhelmed and slaughtered down to the last man.

Paulinus knew he was facing a desperate situation. Two out of the four legions at his disposal were effectively out of action. Half the IX legion had been slaughtered, and the II legion was in distant Exeter, and not responding to pleas for help. The Romans were spread out far too thinly around the province of Britannia. It is not clear that why they had not anticipated such an uprising, and how they had allowed themselves to become so vulnerable. Their odds of victory were slim. Failure to stop the rebellion would mean the end of Roman rule in Britain, and the certain death of almost every Roman remaining in the province. Indeed, Paulinus did not have the luxury of simply absconding back to Gaul as Decianus did. He knew that he had to stand and fight.

The notion that Boudicca had 100,000 men under her command, and that this quickly swelled to 230,000 is questionable. In reality, Boudicca could not possibly feed and water a standing army of that size. Paulinus had at most 12,000 men under his command, and they were massively outnumbered. However well-trained and equipped his troops were, it is unlikely that they could withstand guerrilla ambushes or facing the rebels on an open plain with such large numbers. Paulinus needed more time; the notion of a sustained rapid march to meet with Boudicca's multitude is questionable. By staying in one place rather than actively hunting for the British masses, Paulinus had ensured that his legionaries were rested, well fed, and ready for battle. His forces would not be at risk of surprise guerrilla attacks while on the march and he could organise his auxiliary forces more effectively. Thus, Paulinus would need to plan this battle thoroughly.

Whilst Caesar was said to be a risk taker, (Hoffmann 65) Paulinus certainly was not. Indeed, Tacitus called Paulinus 'the prudent'. And although both were successful generals, Paulinus' successes seem to have been down to him following the Roman military text-books to the letter. And now Paulinus, facing a very large opponent had to follow his predecessor's examples of how to deploy against overwhelming odds. His battle plan would take into account he was outnumbered. He had no choice but to depend on his artillery to be able to keep his casualty rates down. Despite all these measures, Paulinus knew that he still only had a slim chance of victory, He did not have the luxury of sending highly trained and valuable troops into battle without careful planning. As Waite points out, legionnaires were very different to the 'munition fodder' of the First World War, in which commanders thoughtlessly sent tens of thousands of young men 'over the top' in futile assaults, only to be mown down by enemy machine guns. Paulinus and his senior staff knew that they could not just order their legionnaires to make a conventional charge at a much larger enemy. They needed to carefully assess their enemy's strengths and weaknesses and use tactics that would result in fewer casualties. In the unlikely event that they would emerge victorious in this conflict, he would need a strong, standing force to curtail any secondary reprisals. Therefore, only a full-frontal assault on his positions was his only chance of victory. Should he fail, would mean the end of the Roman occupation. Therefore, the 'battle strategy and location would be critical factors before they could allow any confrontation to take place.

The Roman Empire was hugely successful, and credit has to be given to the military strategy and expertise of its generals. Although they had their fair share of failures, they did not take defeat lightly. Indeed, they pursued Hannibal, Spartacus and Vercingetorix relentlessly.

Julius Caesar, is perhaps the most famous of the Roman generals. He was a very astute battle commander. He was said to out-manoeuvre and out-think most of his opponents. Yet, he was not the most successful of all the Roman generals. Caesar fought 43 battles and lost 5. Yet there were several other commanders who were equally as adept as the great Caesar. Gnaeus Pompeius Magnus or Pompey the Great, became very rich by his exploits. His conquests in the east brought enormous wealth to Rome (Roff 106) but, the most successful general was Publius Cornelius Scipio who never lost a battle. He was so successful he was awarded the surname Africanus after the battle of Zama in 202 BC. Yet, they all had one thing in common, and that was choosing the right ground before accepting combat.

Scipio Africanus had no time for ill-prepared officers. He believed any military campaign should only be conducted after exhaustive preparation and planning had been undertaken. (Bédoyère 141) Scipio's actions steered the Romans to be masters at military strategy resulting in many writings about it. In the first century AD Onasander, the Greek philosopher, wrote *Duties of a General* about Roman army tactics. In the fourth century Pubilius Vegetius Renatus penned *De*

Re Militari, a treatise about Roman military tactics throughout the centuries. They both wrote about the importance of fighting on open ground for cavalry to enable cut up of the enemy, particularly during the flight; and about how holding high ground allowed the greater use of artillery weapons such as javelins, arrows and slingshot to be thrown with greater force and made it more difficult for the enemy to engage while scaling a hill.

All such works stress the importance of choosing favourable ground for any campaign, and how to use natural features to protect an army particularly when outnumbered by a greater adversary. Indeed, Julius Caesar was very experienced at overcoming larger enemy forces by the skilful use of terrain. The term 'favourable ground' is often mentioned in his writings; on several occasions Caesar was known to avoid or delay battle because he was not happy with the layout of the land, and it was common for Caesar's units to lie in wait for the enemy at the top of hills or ridges.

Caesar's memoirs mention this tactic several times and in one of Caesar's major battles, at Bibracte in Gaul in 58BC, he deployed his favourite *triple acies* formation halfway down a hillside, with his auxiliaries placed behind an earth fortification at the summit, to defeat a much larger force of Helveti. A few years earlier, at the battle of Pistoria in Italy in 62BC, the Roman Politician, Catiline's outnumbered forces, without any cavalry to protect them, used a defile with steep broken ground on each side to protect their flanks. Although Catiline was defeated during his failed attempt at overthrowing the republic, his use of the geography of the battlefield had delayed the inevitable.

He (Paulinus) would be aware of certain places where ground would counterbalance superiority of numbers.

Tacitus 52

Now that the battle site had been selected, it was time to prepare. Firstly, the Romans needed to fortify the hill and surrounding terrain to prevent any attacks on their flanks. The construction of wooden fortifications, to protect their wings with several rows of *tribuli* - sharpened wooden stakes strapped together in a star formation, several feet high and almost impenetrable to infantry and cavalry–

These rows would begin at the base of the defile and deployed all the way to the top of the escarpment, effectively funnelling the Britons into the defile. The Celt's blind rage towards their invaders let them down as they were herded up the slope for their annihilation.

Anti-slip timber treads set out along the ground half a metre apart to enable the Legionnaires to maintain a solid foot-hold on the slope. These strips were long horizontal branches squared off and fixed perpendicular to the gradient which was fixed into the ground with small stakes to prevent the Legionnaires from slipping during combat. Roman commanders knew that it was vitally important that their Legionnaires remained standing at all times during battle. If they slipped, they would be killed. Visually, this would be similar to a ramp at the rear of a cattle truck and would have enabled soldiers and auxiliary troops to keep a firm footing and enable them to operate with sufficient purchase to flood the Britons with enough weaponry to keep the attacking army at bay.

All of the defences would have been constructed with timber taken locally. As well as food and water, supplies of wood was an essential commodity for the Roman army to operate effectively. Timber was used for fuel and for cooking, metalworking, and as a building material for defence fortifications, dry stores, and shelter for troops and livestock. An army of several thousand troops needed immense amounts of timber. Where an army was dug in and preparing for battle, huge areas of woodland would be cleared and the effect on the landscape could be brutal. (Bédoyére 123) Not only did Paulinus need suitable ground, but he also needed timber and lots of it.

The Romans had to make sure their defences were adequate. They could not take the risk of meeting the British on a flat open plain, they had to rely on natural defences to reinforce any sort of chance of winning. As the battlefield had already been predetermined by Paulinus and his senior advisors, their only problem was how to lure the mighty rebel army to the preferred site.

He [Paulinus] chose a position in a defile with a wood behind him. There could then be, he knew, no enemy, except at his front where lay open country with no cover for ambushes.

(Tacitus, Annals X1V, 34)

Over a hundred years later, at Pascombe Pit, Paulinus was to imitate the tactics of his military predecessors. The Britons, preferring to go into battle semi naked, and sometimes completely naked with their skin died with blue woad would perhaps have helped to put fear into their opponents, particularly, the younger recruits, but the more experienced senior legionnaires on the rear *acies* would have known they were easy targets for their artillery auxiliaries and their Pila. Therefore, the archers, slingers and spearmen would be paying a pivotal role in the early stages of the impending battle. Constant volleys of arrows from the archers would have been relentlessly raining down on the charging Britons, Likewise, the slingers, using either small lead slingshot or small stones would have been used.

The Roman lead sling-shot was a small projectile that resembled a very small lemon and weighed approximately 60 grams. (2 ounces) It had a point at each end, and could travel at speeds up to 100 mph. An experienced slinger could hit a human target at 100 metres and was more accurate than a hand gun over the same distance. At the battle of Mount Gindarus in 38BC it is reported that the expert slingers of Ventidius' army even repelled a cavalry charge. (Cowen p44)

Then there were the Pilum, the heavy spear that were discharged by the front rows to devastating effect, particularly when discharged on a hill. The heavy Pila spear heads consisted of soft, supple iron and were designed to crumple when it penetrated an enemy shield making it difficult to remove it and often forcing the warrior to abandon the shield on the battlefield, thus exposing him further to the torrential rain of artillery volleys and was particularly effective against the Celtic Britons who refused to wear body armour. A continuous barrage of these weapons was crucial for a Roman victory.

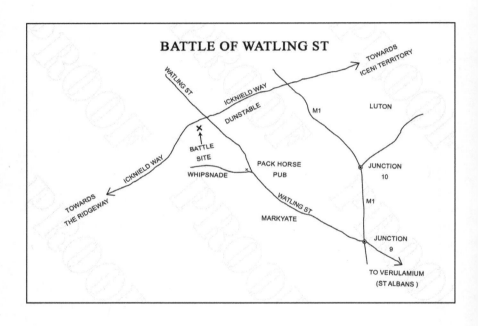

48

5

The Battle of Watling Street

I t is conceivable that the Romans would have been dug-in at Pascombe Pit, prior to the battle and may have been there for weeks beforehand preparing for the clash that mathematically they could not win. In addition, it is contentious to suggest that Paulinus and his Legions arrived on Catuvellauni lands near to Verulamium (St Albans) before Boudicca even reached London. The Romans had wrongly assumed that Boudicca and her rebels would head to Verulamium after razing Camulodunum. (Colchester) But they headed south to Londinium instead, so Paulinus' first task was to stop them from crossing the river at all costs and get them to turn and head back northwest towards Verulamium. Once they reached Verulamium, all he had to do then was to entice them out of the town along Watling Street to the selected battle site on the Dunstable Downs, just northwest of the *colonia*. Here, Paulinus and his remaining two Legions were waiting for them at the junction where, even today two thousand years later is where the Icknield Way crosses Watling Street.

Tacitus writes: "The legionnaires were stationed in close order, with the light armed troops on the flanks and the cavalry massed on the [outer] wings. There were no wings to speak of here as the defile at Pascombe Pit is too narrow to place cavalry on the flanks. Although this was the usual Roman deployment – but, not on this occasion. Paulinus had deployed only a small detachment on the gradient; his remaining forces were out of sight beyond the crest of the escarpment. His tactic was to deploy his youthful IVX Gemima Legion halfway down the slope to tempt the Britons to attack. The Romans always put their youngest, poorest legionnaires at the front, yet the Celts did the opposite, always placing their elite warriors who were mostly from their nobles on the front lines. Unfortunately, when they charged at the almost impenetrable frontal positions of the Roman Legions without adequate armour, they were the first be cut down, leaving the rear of untrained farmers, townsfolk, labourers and serfs at the mercy of the more experienced Legionnaires a few *acies* back.

With most of the Roman strength safely hidden from view, only the legionnaires from the XIV Gemima were visible to the Britons at this time, and even then, not all of them. The rest of Paulinus' forces, including the more experienced XX Legion and auxiliary cavalry, would have been well out of sight awaiting their orders to mobilise. Consequently, the Britons expected a 'walk-over' as all they could see was a small number of troops deployed and many of the young Celtic warriors were tempted to attack without warning. They assumed that the Roman presence at Pascombe Pit was merely a small marching camp, without hardly any cavalry, and one that they could easily vanquish. Unfortunately, due to their recent successes, they now thought they were invincible and could easily defeat any Roman force they came up against. Gradually, tens of thousands of the Britons were congregating on the plain at the foot of the defile. Wave after wave of fighters were arriving from the Watling Street – Icknield Way crossroads and their numbers were quickly intensifying on the plain. Their huge baggage train was pulling up way back around the edge of the flat and due to their numbers, would have been several rows deep. The wagons were full of women, children and as many supplies as they could carry; and they were looking forward to watching the obliteration of more members of the Roman army. Tacitus wrote:

'The forces of the British on the other hand pranced about far and wide in bands of infantry and cavalry, their numbers without precedent and so confident that they brought their wives with them and set them in carts drawn up around the far edge of the battlefield to witness their victory.'

In ancient times it was safer for the women and children to stay with their menfolk, as it was too dangerous for them to remain alone and unprotected at their settlements. They would be open to assaults by neighbouring tribes, roaming militia, or renegade bandits. Many of them could have been displaced off their lands after the killing of their loved ones, or victims of the Roman land grab. The hatred towards the Romans would have been endemic not only by the warriors, but throughout the entire convoy. These women were steadfast supporters of the armed forces they were with and assisted in the daily running of the army by providing meals, washing clothes, feeding the livestock, and nursing the wounded etc. Unfortunately, should their army lose in battle; they were perpetually the victims of unimaginable retribution.

The war chariots carrying the tribal warrior elite were scrambling around the plain at the foot of the defile. Indeed, the chariots were not as extravagant as some scholars would depict and certainly not as flamboyant as the celebrated statue placed on the Thames by the Houses of Parliament by Thomas Thornycroft. Boudicca was said to be in one with her two daughters waving her arms inciting the warriors into a frenzy. The noise from the cumbersome chariots would have been thunderous. The waggons were probably driven by young boys, not ready for combat yet but certainly able to operate the carts carrying the tribal elite to the required areas. The noise was fearsome. Indeed, Caesar mentioned the chariots could generate terror among young enemy ranks:- He wrote:

In chariot fighting the Britons begin by driving all over the field hurling javelins, and generally the terror inspired by the horses and the noise of the wheels are sufficient to throw their opponents' ranks into disorder. Then, after making their way between the squadrons of their own cavalry, they jump down from the chariots and engage on foot. In the meantime, their chariots retire a short distance from the battle and place the chariots in such a position that their masters, if hard pressed by numbers, have an easy means of retreat to their own lines.

Julius Caesar, Gallic Wars IV, 33

Tacitus writes that "Boudicca rode in a chariot with her daughters before her, and as she approached each tribe, she declared that the Britons were accustomed to engage in warfare under the leadership of women. Tacitus claims that Paulinus told them that among the British ranks "there were more women visible than fighting men", as if

51

to calm their panic and to diminish the threat that such a large enemy force presented. The air would have been full of deafening cries from the rebel army, and the sound of Roman swords being bashed against shields.

The elite warriors had now disembarked from their chariots and were now amassing at the foot of the escarpment, just out of range of the artillery. They would be leading the assault up the narrow defile slope on foot. The Romans were still bashing their swords against their shields to demonstrate their antagonism against them and increase the adrenalin among the Roman ranks. The noise would have been resonating around the escarpment and it must have been terrifying for the young Legionnaires on the front acies as they witnessed tens of thousands of warriors amassing below them. As their numbers continued to swell, Paulinus was said to try and calm the terror among the younger fighters on the front lines by rallying his troops. He appeared at the crest of the defile and surveyed the rebels amassing below whilst displaying his arrogance towards them to keep morale high. Then, a quick glance to his left, and then his right, and then behind him. They were ready as they would ever be, yet he would not let his Legions make the first move.

"Ignore the racket made by these savages. There are more women than men in their ranks. They are not soldiers – they are not even properly equipped. We have beaten them before and when they see our weapons and feel our sprit, they will crack. Stick together. Throw the javelin, then push forward; knock them down with your shields and finish them off with your swords. Forget about plunder. Just win and you will have everything."

Would the young Legionnaires have been given something to calm their nerves? Possibly - throughout history the use of drugs to assist in the resolve of men on battlefields is noted. Even in ancient times. Roman medics were aware of the pain killing qualities of poppy seeds, (morphine) There is evidence that drugs were cultivated over 3,500 years ago in the Levant, Egypt and the Middle East. Drugs were also consumed in Britain. Welsh Druids used *amanita muscaria* (the red and white fungi also known as fly agaric, or 'magic mushroom' in their ceremonies. These pretty looking mushrooms are often seen in animated films, and man-made ornaments standing proudly in suburban gardens with a gnome sitting on the top. However, this fungus is hallucinogenic if consumed in large quantities. Roman soldiers meanwhile were known to use cannabis or opium, but they may have consumed mushrooms in Britain as well.

It is believed the Vikings and the Beserkers – (Norse warriors from what we now call Norway), and ancient Britons often consumed these mushrooms before a fight, to dull their fear, make them more ferocious, and blot out physical pain. Indeed, the Beserkers were said to have become so aggressive under the effect of hallucinogenic mushrooms that they even turned on each other after the enemy had been slain and carried on killing everything in their path. However, some scholars have argued that they were not taking magic mushrooms at all but taking Henbane – Stinking Nightshade which put them in an immeasurable rage. An Icelandic poet from the 13th century – possibly Egil Skallagrimsson once wrote of a typical Beserker:

..a demoniacal frenzy suddenly took him; he furiously bit and devoured the edges of his shield; he kept gulping down fiery coals; he snatched live embers in his mouth and let them pass down into his entrails; he rushed through the perils of crackling fires; and at last, when he had raved through every sort of madness, he turned his sword with raging hand against the hearts of six of his champions. It is doubtful whether this madness came from thirst for battle or natural ferocity.

Ranker.com/list/Viking-beserker-facts/philgibbins

Henbane seeds were discovered in a Viking grave in Fykat, Denmark in 1977 which fortifies the suggestion of drug use, and it is widely accepted that the Druids in ancient Britain used hallucinogenic mushrooms during their rituals. But drug use among Roman Legionnaires and ancient Britons is subject to hearsay, however, it cannot be ruled out.

Julius Caesar's favourite formation was the *triplex acies*, in which Roman soldiers stood in three rows, moving forward or backwards so each row could use their different weapons to best effect [ii]. But on this occasion, Paulinus would need a dense deployment to resist the high-volume rebel charge. Others have suggested that Paulinus may have used the *cuneus* (pig's head) configuration: a dense formation used to crash through thin enemy lines. But as the Roman force was so much smaller than the British one, Paulinus knew he did not have the luxury of using these conventional tactics, which would not have stood much of a chance of withstanding a relentless charge by tens of thousands of warriors.

Therefore, the legionaries that were positioned on the defile slope would almost certainly have been deployed in the *Phalanx* formation for this confrontation. Men arranged in close formation - shoulder to shoulder in files stretching across the defile and right up to the *tribuli* defences that had previously been erected all around the base of the hill with further tiers spread all the way up the slope to the summit that would effectively funnel the rebels into the defile.

It would have been prudent for the lines (acies) to be armed with Sarrisa pikes - spears 4-6 meters long and almost impossible to penetrate particularly on a slope. The back lines would have their pikes upright in wait for their deployment. This formation was favoured by the Macedonians and used extensively by Alexander the Great and was sometimes adopted by the Romans as a defensive configuration rather than an offensive one. The only weakness with the *Phalanx* deployment is that it is vulnerable on its flanks. This was addressed easily by the placement of so much *tribuli* positioned in the narrow defile, and augmented by significant artillery forces of archers and slingers which were positioned safely behind the *tribuli* defences along the ridge of the defile enabling them to operate without the fear of attack.

Each row (acies) would have been two metres apart. If part of the line came under direct attack, legionaries would move closer to each other, and use their shields to protect their neighbours and make the formation harder to penetrate. In addition, the front line of a Roman army formation normally fought for less than ten minutes, until horns sounded and the front acies would then pull back to allow the following acies to move forward to ensure that the battling front lines were never exhausted.

Paulinus' choice of the battle ground at Pascombe Pit had resulted in the use of the rebels' chariots and cavalry ineffectual, as they could only be used at the foot of the slope. As a result, the Romans would not have laid out *Caltrops*, a well-used anti-cavalry defence consisting of small, spiked star formations, with one iron spike always facing upwards. Caltrops were no bigger that a man's hand, but they were lethal to mounted troops and could stop a galloping horse if it stepped on one. However, these anti-cavalry defences could hamper the Romans' own cavalry counter-charges, which by now, had already been planned, so they too would be of little use in this battle.

The warriors were now ready, thousands of them shouting and chanting, the noise from both sides would have carried for miles. The rebels, edging ever closer to the foot of the hill were testing the resolve of the Roman lines. Here, it would have been foolish for the Romans to take the bait and make the opening move. They had to remain within the protected area of the defile due to the immense numbers that they faced.

Suddenly, the rebels charged at the hill, racing each other to see who could get to the Romans first. The roar from the warriors would have put fear into the front ranks. Tacitus wrote:

At first, the Legion did not move from its position and kept to the narrow confines of the defile as its protection.

(Tacitus X1V 37))

The warriors, in their extreme rage did not realise that they were being herded in like sheep into their pens. The huge numbers rushing at the defile began to close-in on each other. Because of the narrowness of Pascombe Pit and the deployment of the defensive *tribuli*, only a certain amount of the vast rebel army could confront the Romans at any one time. They were now so close to each other, that using their weapons would be restrictive.

The Celts reached the base of the slope and began to scale the lower slope as fast as they could, shields in one hand, and their mighty swords in the other; then, they encountered another defensive ploy.

55

They were totally unaware that the Romans had been soaking the lower incline for days to make it a slippery slope and made the hill almost inaccessible from the base. As they reached the soaked areas shouting and screaming at the terrified young legionnaires, suddenly they were slipping over and unable to remain standing. Immediately, the slingers and archers moved forward along the ridgelines on both sides and showered the unprotected warriors with a deluge of artillery. As the Britons put their hands out forward to protect their fall and their refusal to wear armour ensured complete carnage. Thousands of slingshot and arrows were now raining down. The warriors were at the mercy of the artillery now, arrows thumping into their exposed bodies and slingshot piercing their skin on their backs, legs, chests and heads. It was a turkey shoot and the beginning of a dreadful slaughter. The initial stages of the battle would have seen much bloodshed on the Boudican side. The Roman front lines were not going to be penetrated here and were now taking control. In just a matter of less than an hour, the advantage of the rebels' immense numbers had been reduced drastically. Tightly packed in and being rained on by javelins, arrows and slingshot, the rebel forces sustained heavy losses, and started to panic. A stampede would have occurred, with the Britons falling over each other as they tried to retreat out of the defile towards the plain. Unfortunately, like most stampedes, there would have been fatalities here too.

Safely behind the Roman lines there would be the Roman supply train, from which the slave runners were constantly racing back and forth from the supply wagons refilling the quivers of the archers with thousands of arrows and slingshot for the slingers who were continuing their blanket artillery volleys. Ancient armies often dipped the ends of projectiles in animal faeces to encourage infection, and in the days before antiseptics and penicillin, septicity would have taken its toll on an abundant number of the walking wounded ensuring a slow and painful death.

Horns sounded, and the auxiliary sections ceased their onslaught and the Phalanx formation edged forwards, still with their pikes protruding, treading on the dead and the dying using them as secure footholds over the quagmire, every other *acies* systematically stabbing and spearing the bodies underfoot as the main bulk of attackers retreated back down the hill. The remaining Legionnaires of the IVX were mobilised and appeared at the crest of the defile and began their descent to join in the melee. Then, the XX Legion came into sight, and equally began their descent. Shields held firmly against their bodies and their Gladius swords at the ready, the slaughter was certainly not over yet. Close quarter hand-to-hand fighting continued at the base of the hill and now the Romans were winning the day. This resulted in most of the elite warriors being either dead or seriously wounded and the rest of the untrained warriors were to look on in horror as they witnessed another couple of thousand troops descending the slope to join the conflict.

During this onslaught, the rebels failed to notice the cavalry sections racing south along the top of the escarpment to the rear of the plain. The Celts now faced squares of experienced Legionnaires at their front and then thousands of cavalry were galloping across the plain to attack them from their rear.

The use of pikes is further supported in the *Works of Tacitus* translated by Arthur Murphy:

'The cavalry, at the same time bore down upon the enemy, and with their pikes, overpowered all who dared to make a stand.'

The thousand horse cavalry section reached the baggage train first and began spearing all and sundry. The rebels were running back to the train in search of their loved ones as naturally they would not have wanted to flee without them. But they were completely exposing themselves and their families to the mercy of their adversaries. Paulinus and his commanders were now openly in control and orchestrating their manoeuvres due to their excellent views of the land below them and directing their forces accordingly. It was here that the cavalry took over to finally slaughter the remaining fleeing fighters and the Legionnaires then set their sights on the baggage train full of women and children. The carnage must have been appalling.

The women and children would have been slaughtered just as mercilessly as the men. Tacitus writes. 'The Roman soldiers did not refrain from slaughtering even the womenfolk, while the baggage animals too, transfixed with weapons, added to the piles of bodies.... For some there are who record that almost 80,000 Britons fell, while Roman casualties amounted to some 400 dead and a similar number wounded.'

Dio says the battle was all over in a couple of hours, maybe less. Paulinus' choice of battlefield had turned out to be a stroke of genius. Not only did the Romans have the advantage of being on the top of a steep hill. When the British retreated, they had no option but to flee out onto an open plain, where they were easily cut to pieces by the pursuing cavalry. If Boudicca's forces had adopted Caractacus' guerrilla tactics the result could have been very different. If they had planned their assault on the Romans properly, their superior numbers would probably have prevailed. If they had besieged the ridge, or mounted a guerilla campaign of attrition, they may have worn the Romans down, and that might have convinced emperor Nero to abandon Britain indefinitely. Instead, they had allowed themselves to be lured into a defile and mounted a foolhardy charge up one of the steepest hillsides in southern England. Their victories in Colchester, London and St Albans had made them over-confident, and their thirst for Roman blood had put them off guard. They had fallen willingly into a Roman deception.

6

In Search of The Defile

The search for the defile has eluded academics, historians, archaeologists, and amateur sleuths for many generations. The scant clues that the Roman historians left is all we have to go on. But the description of a narrow defile with deep sides may be a mistranslation that the battle was fought on very hilly ground. Given that Paulinus's forces were so heavily outnumbered, it would make sense for him to have chosen a site where steep slopes, hilltops and narrow valleys could be turned to his advantage and shorten his odds of victory. But where is it?

Both Tacitus and Dio's accounts of the Boudiccan uprising agree on the route that Boudicca and her rebels took. We can be sure that her forces burned Camulodunum (Colchester) first, then Londinium (London), and then Verulanium (St Albans). Although Dio only references two settlements in his *Roman Histories*, - and does not name them, it is likely that he is referring to Camulodunum and Verulanium as Londinium at that time was not ranked as a town during the 60 – 61AD uprising. While both Camulodunum and Verulanium were *colonia.*, that is, the two towns were officially Roman settlements.

There is no mention of any more towns being attacked, and after St Albans the archaeological trail is fruitless. But, this hasn't stopped most scholars to assume that Boudicca's forces carried on in a north-westerly direction from St Albans, up Watling Street (or the Celtic track that preceded it), until she encountered the Romans somewhere in the midlands.

The number of potential battle sites that are backed up by serious research has now grown well into double figures; and several more have emerged without any supporting evidence whatsoever. Some modern writers about Roman historians have simply sidestepped the question of the battle's location. Vanessa Collingridge's 2005 book *Boudicca* runs through many possible sites, without expressing a preference. Charlotte Higgins' book *Under Another Sky: Journeys in Roman Britain*, published in 2014, concludes that the battle must have been "somewhere near London". But most other writers have named a place. As Higgins has said, "There is no evidence, but there has been plenty of fantasy".

Two of the more plausible theories assume that Boudicca headed a long way north of St Albans, well into the Midlands, before she was defeated. The late Graham Webster, a well-respected archaeologist, spent many years advocating Mancetter (Manduessedum), a small village right on Watling Street, in what Webster calls the "central Midlands": north Warwickshire, not far from the Leicestershire border. Webster first made the case for Mancetter in his 1978 book *Boudicca: The British Revolt Against Rome, AD60*. More recently Margaret Hughes, a writer from the nearby town of Atherstone, has also argued in its favour[i].

The terrain around Mancetter certainly looks plausible. This part of Warwickshire is surprisingly hilly. Mancetter itself is on the river Anker, and just to the south of the village the land rises steeply to a ridge. There has been lots of quarrying around Mancetter over the centuries, but 2,000 years ago there may have been jagged outcrops of Hartshill stone on the ridge line, making the area seem much craggier, and 'defile-like', than it does today. There is a hollow in the steep slopes of the ridge, which may be the defile that Tacitus describes.

Webster's hypothesis is that the Roman army did not have time to head any further south than Mancetter after news of Boudicca's rebellion reached Anglesey, and that after sacking St Albans, Boudicca's forces headed 80 miles northwards up Watling Street to confront them. Some have suggested that Manduessedum is a Latinisation of an old Celtic name meaning 'place of the chariot', and that it was so named because Boudicca's army, and its chariots fought there. Furthermore, an important Roman vexillation fortress – a 25-acre, rectangular fortress seems to have been set up at Mancetter in the middle of the first century. It may have been established when Paulinus mustered there to fight the Britons, or soon after Boudicca's defeat, to keep the peace in the area.

However, the problem with Mancetter is that there's very little archaeological evidence of a battle being fought there. Only a single Pilum spearhead has ever been found. At the base of the ridge, the river Anker would have been wide and marshy 2,000 years ago, and it may have impeded the Roman's pursuit of the retreating British and made it easier for them to escape unscathed. In 2012-13 Alan Cook, a geologist living near Mancetter, started testing soil samples across a wide area – stretching as far as Nuneaton, Hinckley and Tamworth - to look for traces of iron, lead, zinc, tin and copper, which would have been left by a huge battle. Cook identified 24 kilometre squares which had an abnormally high level of metal, but no clear evidence of weapons has yet emerged.

Today Mancetter has a Boudicca Heritage Centre, but even Webster himself described Mancetter as merely a "distinct possibility" and "a best guess" as the site of the battle. Although Webster advanced a good argument that Mancetter was an important military camp, his argument that it was also an important battlefield is less convincing.

High Cross, a village on Watling Street 10 miles south-east of Mancetter, has been strongly advocated by John Waite, in his book *Boudica's Last Stand.* Waite has argued that High Cross, which is nowadays a small village where the B4455 meets the A5 in Leicestershire, is an obvious place for a battlefield, as it was (or later became) the main crossroads of Roman Britain, where Watling Street and the Fosse Way crossed. Waite claims that after burning down St Albans' Boudicca's forces were intent on doing the same at Ratae *Corieltavorum* (Leicester), and that they marched up Watling Street to High Cross, at which they were planning to turn right onto Fosse Way, which would lead them directly to Ratae. Originally a British settlement and the base of the Coritani tribe, Ratae had been established as a Roman town in 44AD and was already an important commercial and military centre, whose defences were improved in around 61AD (possibly to deter an attack by Boudicca's forces, though all historians agree that she never reached the town). Waite has suggested that Boudicca may have wanted to seek an alliance with the Coritani (and possibly the Parisi, another tribe in what we now call East Yorkshire) to secure victory over the Romans.

Paulinus' forces, meanwhile, marched down to High Cross from Mancetter, the nearest big military base to Leicester, to head Boudicca off[ii]. Waite believes that Paulinus would not have headed any further south down Watling Street towards London as he did not want to venture too far from Mancetter and other big Roman military bases in the north and west Midlands. High Cross's location at a crossroads gave Paulinus lots of options should he fail in battle and need to retreat quickly.

So far, so good. The big problem with High Cross is that the land there is a flat plateau, or what Waite inventively calls a 'gently contoured ridge'. It may have far-reaching views today, suggesting that Paulinus would have seen the enemy coming, but 2,000 years much of the land would be covered in dense woodland. Even if there was a clearing, it would have been flat land – exactly the kind of terrain that Paulinus would have avoided, for fear of being surrounded by the Britons and wiped out.

Waite claims that the battle was fought just north of the crossroads, and that Paulinus could have funnelled the British forces towards him by ditches and banks on either side of his formations (evidence of the western earthworks has been found, but not the eastern ones). Some way to the west of his proposed battle site is Smockington Hollow, a pronounced dip in the terrain. Unlike most other historians Waite argues that this hollow, or defile, was not where the British were lured to be slaughtered, but a hiding place in which Paulinus's reserve forces were concealed from the unsuspecting Britons.

There is some local archaeology: at Wigston Parva, a hamlet less than a mile north of High Cross, are the remains of semi-permanent' Roman fort, astride the course of Watling Street, which indicates that it must have been constructed before the road, possibly as accommodation for its builders, or the soldiers who defended them. Waite points to the evidence of another 'marching camp' nearby, which may have been used by the Romans before or after the battle. But there isn't any clear archaeological evidence at High Cross, apart from what Waite vaguely calls "clear marks and features which may suggest that Roman forces not only made temporary camps in the area but also carried out some type of engineering work". As at Mancetter, no weapons or human remains have been found.

Further south, in Northamptonshire, two possible battles sites have been put forward. The first is Cuttle Mill, favoured by the military historian Martin Matrix-Evans, and which lies right on Watling Street. Matrix-Evans argues that Paulinus was defending Towcester (Lactodurum), which was the next town of any consequence on Watling Street north of Verulamium. (St Albans) But Matrix-Evans concedes that his case is based on little more than ancient local folklore about a battle having taken place there, and an unauthorised dig for Roman gold in the 1930s (none was found). Not far away is the village of Church Stowe, favoured by the Harvard archaeologist John Pegg, who argues that Boudicca had been planning to use the nearby Nene Valley as a route back to east Anglia after defeating the Romans. There certainly is evidence of Roman ditches and banks in the area, In the 1840s human bones were found nearby, and a horseshoe much smaller than common in modern Britain. But no more signs of a battlefield have been found.

It is the same story at Clifton-upon-Dunsmore, a small village just north-east of Rugby, and only a mile west of Watling Street. The village is on a low ridge, facing northwards towards the river Avon, but the ridge cannot be said to have any narrow defiles. Those who favour Clifton-upon-Dunsmore rely heavily on a possible connection between Boudicca and the legend of the Dun Cow, from which the Dunsmore part of the village name might be derived. In a similar vein, an amateur historian Martyn Tagg has suggested that the battle took place in Oxfordshire at the Roman settlement of Alchester, where the town of Bicester now stands[iii]. But the land around Bicester is mostly very flat, with no'defile' nearby.

Much nearer to Verulamium (St Albans) the archaeologist Grahame Appleby has suggested Arbury Banks, **an** ancient hill fort dating back to the Bronze Age (1000 – 700BC) just outside Ashwell, a village four miles north of Baldock in Hertfordshire. Appleby has argued that the Romans could have adapted the old hill fort into a stronghold from which to defend against the Britons. There are traces of a Roman building nearby, and Appleby has argued that it could have been a temple built to celebrate the Romans' victory.

The hillfort certainly has quite a narrow entrance, only 300 metres wide, into which the British forces could be funnelled. The hillfort lies in rolling terrain with a 'dry valley', at the far eastern end of the Chiltern Hills, though there is no defile as such. It is possible that the British stumbled upon the Roman army at Arbury Banks while marching back towards Norfolk and Suffolk along the Icknield Way (which passes near Ashwell) after their sacking of St Albans, which is about 20 miles away to the south-west. Although Arbury Banks has its merits, there needs to be more substantial archaeological evidence before it is to be considered seriously.

Even closer to St Albans is Dunstable, which is today the first town on Watling Street northwest of St Albans. From the late 1960s onwards Barry Horne, an archaeologist who lived locally, argued that the Battle of Watling Street took place at Turnpike Farm, just off Watling Street two miles south-east of Dunstable. The site is near the present-day Horse and Jockey pub, halfway between the villages of Caddington and Kensworth. At Kensworth is the source of the River Ver, which Roman forces might have used as a water supply.

Barry Horne's theory relies heavily on a speculative timeline of events. He believes that the two armies probably met head-on 18 or 19 days into the uprising, and three or four days after the British had sacked St Albans – which could be correct. Like others, he believed that the Iceni and Trinovantes may have wanted to head back towards East Anglia on the Icknield Way, which passes through the area. It would make sense for Paulinus to stop the British there, before they turned eastwards towards their tribal lands, or sought sanctuary in the boggy lands of the Fens, where defeating them would be nigh-on impossible.

Horne concluded, probably rightly, that the battle could not have taken place any further north than Dunstable. He asserts that the battle 'probably took place somewhere on or near Watling Stree' but dismisses the idea that it took place in the Midlands. Modern

Dunstable is built on the site of an old Roman settlement: Durocobrivis. This prompts an obvious question: if the battle took place very near a Roman town, why was the town not named in Tacitus's or Dio's accounts of the battle? Horne has a good answer: until the second century AD Durocobrivis was in fact north of present-day Dunstable, in or near the village of Tilsworth. So, in 61AD there was no settlement to speak of where Dunstable now stands.

Sadly, Horne's promising theory begins to fall apart when you look at the site. It is difficult to explore on foot, as most of it is private land without any rights of way. But a drive around the perimeter makes it clear that running through the middle is a wide and shallow valley, with no'defile' in sight. There are no natural features that would have forced the British into a narrow space. Before Barry Horne's death in 2017 the Manshead Archaeology Society, which he ran, was apparently carrying out geophysical surveys using resistivity equipment, but this work seems to have ceased when he died, and no bodies or weapons were ever found.

Then there are further suggestions. The first is Virginia Water in Surrey. Evidence of burning in Putney, Brentford and Staines at around the time of the Boudiccan revolt may mean that some of her forces headed westwards from London to Silchester. There is no certainty over what caused the fires: it could be that Roman buildings were accidentally burned down - thanks to a dropped oil lamp, for example – rather than attacked by marauding tribes. But several historians have suggested that the Romans defeated Boudicca on a battlefield west of London, not north.

Nicholas Fuentes, in his 1985 article *Boudicca Revisited* offered a bold alternative to the received wisdom. Fuentes argues that Paulinus chased the British tribes down the Roman road (known as the Port Way or Devil's Highway) towards Silchester. Fuentes claims that the sacking of St Albans was by "local insurgents", not by the bulk of the British forces, which is scarcely credible, given that both Tacitus and Dio place Boudicca, and most or all her forces there. But Fuentes continues that the British were defeated not in the northern Home Counties or the Midlands, but at Virginia Water, just off the present-day A30 at Runnymede, which closely follows the route of the Roman

Devil's Highway. Paulinus had sought to defeat them there in the hope that it would be easier for reinforcements from the II Legion in Exeter to arrive and bolster his strength.

Fuentes suggests that the battle took place between Callow Hill and Knowle Hill, to the north of the modern settlement of Virginia Water and pointed towards local claims that the site is still haunted by the ghosts of Roman soldiers, probably just another old wives' tale. On inspection of the area, there are some low hills, there are certainly no 'narrow defile'. A map that accompanied Fuentes' article is inaccurate and shows Roman roads in the wrong place relative to the contour lines. Fuentes seems to have tried to persuade readers that Virginia Water is an area of steep-sided hills, but it is not convincing. As at most of other battle sites, no archaeological evidence has been presented, and it would be hard to look for any, given that Virginia Water is home to many wealthy residents who might not take kindly to an army of metal detectorists excavating their grounds.

In 2013 Steve Kaye, a geologist at University College London, published a detailed analysis of the hydrology of southern England in an attempt to pinpoint the battle site using the notion of water consumption for the armies. Kaye argued that given the huge thirst of any large army's soldiers and animals, only a site with access to plenty of water is suitable. Like Nicholas Fuentes, Kaye concluded that Paulinus and his entire army marched to London, and that they then marched westwards, not northwards. But rather than the battle taking place at Virginia Water, Kaye believed that it took place at least 45 miles further west. Paulinus was not pursuing the Britons but heading westwards to avoid annihilation and hoping to reach the relative safety of Roman towns like Cirencester, Gloucester, or even as far as Exeter. This is unlikely, if Paulinus wanted sanctuary, he would have gone south.

Kaye narrowed down a long list of 110 to a shortlist of 40 sites, of which only one (Perry Barr, a suburb of Birmingham) is in the Midlands. Only one (Cockernhoe) is in the Chilterns, and Dunstable is not mentioned. Most of the other sites are either in the Kennet Valley, near Marlborough in Wiltshire, or in the High Cotswolds, near Stow-on-the-Wold. Kaye says his favourite is Ogbourne St George, not far from Marlborough in Wiltshire. Like Fuentes, Kaye does not explain why this is so far from St Albans, the last town that the Britons are reported to have sacked before they were defeated. The British could theoretically have marched the 70 miles from St Albans via the Icknield Way and Ridgeway, but the defile that Kaye pinpoints at Ogbourne is about a kilometre wide, and not very steep-sided, which would have meant the Romans could have easily been surrounded there. It is unlikely that an experienced Roman commander would have chosen it as the battle site.

Even less convincing is the claim that the battle took place nowhere near southern England, but in North Wales. Janet Smart has suggested, in her book entitled *Boudicca: The Truth*, that the Maen Achwyfan Cross, an early memorial that has stood for over a thousand years in a field near the Flintshire village of Whitford, marks the site of the battle. Smart argues that Paulinus never left Wales before he confronted the British, and that Boudicca and her army marched all the way from St Albans to fight the Romans there, which is logistically very unlikely. Boudicca is still very popular with the Welsh people, and she may have had some Welsh ancestry, or ended up in Wales after the battle. But there is no evidence that Boudicca ever fought a battle anywhere in Wales. The Maen Achwyfan Cross has Christian markings and is estimated to have been erected by Vikings nearly 1,000 years after the Boudiccan revolt. Smart argues that the Vikings raised it as a memorial to Boudicca, which is highly improbable. How would the Vikings have known anything about her given that the main written records of her revolt in Tacitus's *Annals*, were lost until the early sixteenth century?

In any case, the immediate surroundings of the cross are quite flat, with no steep-sided defiles. Janet also states that 'an abundance of human and animal remains have been found' over the years, which have evidence of trauma which suggests a battle of some sort occurred there, but there doesn't seem to be any investigations into trying to carbon date them to ascertain the age of the items.

Other suggestions include that the battle took place in central London. The myth that the battlefield was at the village of Battle Bridge, on the old river Fleet, was begun by John Bagford in 1715 after the remains of an elephant were found, alongside a spearhead, in a gravel pit near the Grays Inn Road. Bagford suggested that the elephant was brought over by the Romans and ridden by them in the battle, and the spearhead belonged to one of Boudicca's warriors. However, it has since been discovered that the elephant bones and spearhead (in fact a flint axe head) were Neolithic (and thus several millennia older than the battle), not Roman. The Battle Bridge theory was given new legs by John Nelson's 1811 history of the parish of St Mary's Islington, and by Lewis Spence's 1937 book *Boadicea – Warrior Queen of the Britons*. An urban myth soon spread that Boudicca's body is buried beneath platform 9 or 10 at King's Cross station. This may have been encouraged as a piece of Home Front propaganda during World War Two, a 'heroic myth' to bolster the spirits of Londoners during the Blitz: if Queen Boudicca could vanquish a foreign foe in London, then so could modern Britons. But there is no firm evidence, other than the name Battle Bridge, and no proof that the village derived its name from a battle there. If Boudicca had burned London and then St Albans, why would her army have then gone back to London to fight the Romans?

Another theory is that the battle site, and Boudicca's resting place, is situated on Hampstead Heath, north of London, After the sculptor Thomas Thornycroft's death in 1885 his son John wanted his father's statute of *Boudicca and her Daughters* erected on Boudicca's Mound, a small hill on the heath, where local folklore suggested Boudicca is buried. However, an exploratory dig at the mound found no evidence of her body - only domestic rubbish - so the statue was raised near the Houses of Parliament instead[iv].

None of these suggested battlefields are an exact match with what Tacitus describes as a 'narrow defile'. And it is unlikely that they would have been willingly chosen by Paulinus as a suitable location for a Roman victory. To win, as a force of 10,000 or so against the Britons force that may have been ten or even twenty times bigger, required stringent planning, and a location where it would be difficult for the entire British force to attack at once. But several of the sites are on open plains. If the Roman legions had fought in conventional formations such as the double or triple acies, they would have continually needed to 'wheel' to counter any attacks on their flanks with such overwhelming numbers. Paulinus might have deployed the *Orbis* formation, used in emergencies when a unit was completely surrounded, but his forces would not have lasted long under sustained attack by such a large adversary. The British could easily have completely surrounded the Romans, and they would have probably triumphed.

A battle of this size would have left behind a trail of evidence of weapons, armour, sling-shot, arrowheads and spearheads, pottery and chariots, as well as many bone samples after the site had been stripped. But few items that could be attributed to the Romans or the Britons have been found on any of the sites, items that could have come from Boudicca's army are non-existent.

Pascombe Pit - Dunstable Downs

Pascombe Pit - Dunstable

Dunstable today is just another ordinary town in south Bedfordshire, but on its western edge is one of the most spectacular landscapes in south-east England: the Dunstable Downs. This chalk escarpment in the north-eastern part of the Chilterns is not particularly high, (it is no more than 225 metres above sea level) but is very dramatic, offering panoramic views westwards over the Aylesbury Vale, and northwards over Dunstable towards Milton Keynes and Bedford. The hillsides of the Downs are such that in the eighteen and nineteenth century, local people used to roll oranges down the slopes every Good Friday, with a contest to see who could catch them before they reached the bottom.

Pascombe Pit is part of this escarpment here, (the hill is not named on maps) and not too far from Barry Horne's suggestion along the A5 Watling Street. Travelling out of St Albans towards Dunstable you get the town centre where you reach a crossroads. That junction is an ancient crossroads where the Icknield Way crosses Watling Street. Turn left into Icknield Way towards Ivinghoe and the plain at the base of the defile is a few hundred metres on the left-hand side.

To the rear of the field is the narrow defile in a horse-shoe shape with rising high sides, and it would have been an ideal site to protect an ancient army's flanks. The centre of the slope starts off gradually at the base and then gets quite steep as you reach the top.

The word 'pit' and the site's steep inclines, mean that many people assume it is an old quarry. In fact, it is a completely natural amphitheatre, not a man-made one. Just north of the pit the land rises to a height of 220 metres, and from the hilltop there are 360-degree clear views in all directions. This hill is a natural fortress, and it meant that Paulinus stood zero risk of being surrounded. Looking down from the top of the defile out onto the large plain at the base, it is easy to see how Boudicca's rebel army were funnelled up by their blind rage and inherent hatred of the invaders, they were oblivious to the trap the Romans had set. The plain stretches out a considerable distance and again you can see it is more than capable of holding Boudicca's large baggage train of thousands of people where Tacitus says the

71

non-combatants gathered to witness the assumed annihilation of the Roman forces. It is here that Boudicca's fallen army may have been left as carrion prey after the bloodbath.

The soil is thin and chalky, so it is unlikely that to have had much woodland on it two thousand years ago. The river Ouzel rises near the foot of the escarpment just to the west at a hamlet called Wellhead. The Ouzel then flows northwards, through the modern settlements of Leighton Buzzard and Milton Keynes, to join the Great Ouse at Newport Pagnell. Although the upper part of the Ouzel is little more than a stream now, two thousand years ago many English streams and rivers were bigger due to much more woodland, and more rain than there is today. The Romans would have had a good source of water here for their considerable needs.

The defile was acquired by the Royal Corps of Rifles in 1867 and was used as a rifle-range training ground and it is believed the hill was still used for training during both world wars. Thus, it is of little point carrying out metal detecting on the defile as it is riddled with small munitions. But luckily, only small calibre weapons were ever used here, not heavy artillery, so while the hillside must contain many old bullets, they were never seriously damaged by large shells. Another problem that would affect a survey on the plain, is that when the A41 Berkhamsted bypass was built in the early 1990's the spoil accumulated was brought here and levelled over the plain to level out all the undulations to make it easier for the gliders to take off and land at the London Gliding Club next door.

At the top of the defile is the Five Knolls burial mounds, an ancient burial site and a scheduled monument, which is several millennia older than the Boudicca uprising. It is sobering to realise that the time passed between the first burial at Five Knolls and the battle is much greater than the period between the battle and today. Five Knolls is a misleading name though. There are in fact seven knolls: two bowl barrows, three bell barrows, and two pond barrows. There are also a further two long 'pillow' mounds nearby, which are assumed to be medieval rabbit warrens. The area was excavated in the 1850's and again in the 1920's, when over 90 skeletons from various periods were found, from the latter Neolithic period onwards, including some that could be Roman. The pond barrows look like shallow, grassed craters, which arguably could be where cremations took place. Pliny the Elder wrote that by the 1st century AD, the Romans began to cremate their battle fallen because the enemy were returning to desecrate the remains of the battle dead as soon as the armies had left the area.

There is evidence of a Roman villa on the other side of Icknield Way, though it was probably constructed many years after the Boudicca revolt. The plain at the bottom is owned by two separate farmers who seem to be very reluctant to get involved in any investigations to ascertain whether it could be the actual battle site or not. The actual defile of Pascombe Pit itself is part of the Dunstable Downs and is owned and maintained by the National Trust and is an area of outstanding natural beauty (AONB) You can visit the defile from the top of the escarpment only as the plain at the base is private property. There are large car parks up there (not free) and a cafeteria where you can sit and enjoy the views.

[i] See https://atherstone.nub.news/ news/ local-news/ atherstone- historian-margaret- ughes-ill-be-the- last- woman- standing-in- proving-mancetter-was-where- Boudicca-fought-her- final-battle.

[ii] Waite dismisses the case for Mancetter itself as the site of the battle, as he thinks that the "defiles" in the hillside there would have been too small for the Roman forces to hide in: he assumes that the Romans were lying in wait inside a gorge or narrow valley, not on the ridges above one.

[iii] See https://boudiccaslostbattlefield.com/main-article/.

[iv] See https://lostcityoflondon. co.uk/2018/07/23/ boudiccas -grave/.

Peter Sweeney

Cucle tracks over the burial mounds

7

Outcome

T he Battle of Watling Street was not a spur-of-the-moment engagement, or a chance encounter between two armies wandering around Bedfordshire looking for each other, it was a meticulously planned and brilliantly executed Roman entrapment by one of the most underestimated generals of the Roman Empire.

Surprisingly, Suetonius Paulinus did not emerge from his victory over the British rebels covered in glory. Given that Paulinus was more responsible for the Romans' enduring control of Britannia than anyone else, it is surprising that he was not welcomed back to Rome as a hero, and it is just as surprising that he is not better-known today. Against all the odds, he had defeated a vast Celt army over 10 times bigger than his own. The Celts could easily have been triumphant if they had used guerrilla tactics, but instead Paulinus had lured them to a battlefield of his choosing, where their superior discipline, training and equipment was used to devastating effect. Paulinus had turned an impending slaughter of Roman forces into a triumphant Roman victory and kept his casualties to a minimum.

Within a year or so he was recalled to Rome, amidst suggestions that his brutal crackdown against the Celt warriors who had survived the slaughter of the Battle of Watling Street went too far. Indeed, he was well known for his suppression of the tribes. Dio claims, he was unnecessarily antagonising the ancient Britons and making future uprisings more likely, not less. Paulinus seems to have been judged to be too hard-line a military commander, even by Roman standards to achieve a long-term peace.

Britain's new procurator, Julius Classicanus – Decianus' replacement, is said by Tacitus to have been "on bad terms" with Paulinus, and to have "allowed his personal animosity to stand in the way of the national interest". In the end, it was Paulinus, not Classicanus, who was moved on. Classicanus, Tacitus claims, was "giving out that it would be well to await a new governor who would deal gently with those who surrendered, without feelings of enmity and anger or the arrogance of a conqueror". Classicanus sent a message to Rome, saying that "they should expect no end to hostilities unless a replacement was found for Paulinus, whose failures he attributed to the man's incompetence, his successes to chance".

A freed slave, Polyclitus, was sent from Rome to see if he could effect a reconciliation between Paulinus and Classicanus, and report back to emperor Nero. Polyclitus was apparently treated with derision by both Romans and the Britons, and the latter were "amazed that a general and an army that had carried through so great a war would yield obedience to slaves," Dio claims. Paulinus remained in post for a short while, but he was soon recalled to Rome, possibly in late 62AD, ostensibly because "he lost a few ships",

After Paulinus's departure the new governor of Britain, a consul named Publius Petronius Turpilianus, gave out amnesties and pardons to Britons instead of slaughtering them. Paulinus was to become a consul in Rome in 69 AD, during the War of the Four Emperors that followed the death of Nero, and soon found himself on the losing side, but was granted a pardon. What became of him after that is not known and he vanishes from history.

There are no surviving contemporary accounts of the Romans' victory at the Battle of Watling Street. It may be that there were more immediate, journalistic accounts, which have been lost in the two millennia since. But another possibility is that the battle was not written about much at the time because it was not as total a victory as later generations of historians would claim. Even if it was a glorious success, the fact that for several weeks Celtic forces had been able to wander around southern Britain unchecked, and destroyed three towns without hindrance, was an embarrassment to the Romans. The rebellion was mostly prompted by Roman administrators' demands for the repayment of loans, and unnecessary humiliation of the Iceni and Trinovantes tribes. Maybe the Romans had received more of a bloody nose than was later claimed and had continued to suffer attacks by troublesome tribes even after Boudicca's army was defeated. The full truth may have been censored, or covered up, to prevent a backlash of opinion from Roman citizens, and emperor Nero, and to save Britain's administrators from criticism and disgrace. Later historians may have deliberately downplayed the extent of Roman losses, both in the towns that the British destroyed and in the final battle, to repair wounded Roman pride.

Despite their superior numbers, the Britons suffered a tragic defeat, and the classical writers inform us that up to 80,000 Celts perished at the battle site while the number of Roman dead stood at only 400 with the same amount injured. Many thousands of the Celts would have been wounded on the battlefield and summarily executed by the Romans along with the women, children and livestock that would be of no use to them. The younger women and girls would have been subjected to horrific rape and torture. Should any of the females be with their children, they would have been forced to witness their decapitation before being repeatedly raped themselves. The unlucky ones would have been taken into slavery. The Roman slaves would have to continue with clearing the battlefield witnessing the constant screams, sobs and agonising torture which would have lasted for days. The Romans called the ancient Britons barbarians, they were no better, if not worse, and, it is disturbing to comprehend that, 2000 years later in the 21st century, this sort of behaviour is not left to history but happens around the world even today.

It would have taken days for the slaves to clear the battlefield. The Roman dead were stripped and unceremoniously dragged up the slope by the pack animals to be cremated in the pond barrows at the top of the defile before their ashes were interred in the burial mounds. Retrieving the thousands of arrows, Pila and slingshot artillery that could be reused would have taken considerable time and effort to recover them. This was essential to prevent them from falling into enemy hands. Any food producing stock such as chickens, turkeys or geese would have been allowed to run free until they were herded up for consumption for the Roman war machine and any fodder taken for their own considerable livestock. Their remaining wagons would have been destroyed where they stood. Boudicca's warriors, meanwhile, would have been left where they had fallen, for nature to recycle. Pliny explains that the Romans had very little regard for the bodies of dead enemies, other than their commanders. It is probable that the remains of the fallen were stripped of all belongings and left naked and open to the elements for months, or even years, serving as carrion prey before finally decomposing and being ploughed into the fields over the ages.

The official number of Roman dead is regarded by some as an under-estimate, given that they were attacked by an unrealistic army of up to 230,000 Britons[iii]. But in ancient times it was common for a victorious army to suffer a casualty rate of only 5%, so if the Romans had about 10,000 troops the figures that Tacitus and Dio give (400 dead, and a similar number of wounded) might just be plausible. Paulinus had to use tactics that would have resulted in fewer casualties for his troops. Many scholars have put forward theories that the number of 80,000 Britons lost against just 400 Roman dead and the same number injured are unreliable. However, using his select choice of battle ground and utilizing the artillery sections along with good defence positions would greatly assist in keeping his casualty figures to a minimum. With this in mind, the figures could be realistic. Tacitus refers to more troops being sent from Germany to Britain after the rebellion, to replace the 2,000 legionaries of the IX legion who had been slaughtered on their way to Colchester, but there is no mention of any of the other three legions in Britain being replenished.

The first consequence of the British defeat was a swift expansion of the Roman military domination of southern Britain. The Lunt Fort, near Coventry, may have been set up as a direct result of the Britons' defeat, as a place to keep all the horses that the Romans had captured. Paulinus is said to have gone up to Iceni settlements in Norfolk - at Thetford and Caistor St Edmund to kill more Iceni and deter any further rebellion.

Although the reckoning of Paulinus may have been harsh, it is doubtful that it resulted in many thousands more Iceni deaths as some historians claim. There is no evidence of a large drop in their population. In fact, the harshest consequences may have been borne not by the Iceni but by the Trinovantes. In the end it seems that it was only the Trinovantes themselves who suffered the consequences of this protest. Cassius Dio does not mention the Trinovantes in his accounts of the Boudiccan revolt, and afterwards there are very few historical references to the Trinovantes at all. It may be that they ultimately merged with the Catuvellauni when they lost much of their lands and indeed, their capital: Camulodunum (Colchester) to the Roman settlers and did so in order to survive.

Another immediate consequence of the Roman's victory was, oddly enough, a Roman suicide. Poenius Postumus, the camp prefect of the II Augusta legion in Exeter, Southwest England, fell on his sword when he heard that the other legions' battle with Boudicca's army had ended in an amazing victory. Suicide was considered by the Romans to be an honourable means of death if the alternative was capture by an enemy. The Carthaginian general Hannibal killed himself with poison in 183 BC in Bithynia (the northern coast of modern-day Turkey) to avoid falling into Roman hands. His suicide did not diminish the grudging respect that the Romans had for him as a military commander. Why then would Roman historians invent a story that Boudicca perpetrated her own suicide, and thus make her into a more honourable adversary? It is arguable that the story was invented to cover up the more embarrassing truth: Boudicca somehow escaped the battlefield alive.

It is not clear why Posthumus took responsibility for the II legion's failure to join the battle, as he was only the legion's third in command (the identity of its first and second in command is unknown). The official story, according to Roman historians, is that Postumus had simply disobeyed a direct order to send troops urgently to the aid of the XIV (14th) and XX (20th) legions. As Tacitus puts it:

Poenius Postumus, camp prefect of the Second Legion which had not joined Paulinus, learning of the success of the other two formations, fell on his sword because he had cheated his legion of its share in the victory and broken regulations by disobeying his commander's orders.

(Tacitus, Annals XIV. 37)

79

Both Tacitus and Dio along with modern scholars seem to have judged Posthumus harshly: It was stated that he was guilty of a 'disgraceful failure' to obey a direct order from his most senior commander, Paulinus. But there is a suggestion that the II legion had its hands full in the West Country, dealing with a local rebellion of its own. The legion may have been quite simply unable to leave its fort in Exeter or decided that sending a contingent of valuable troops to rendezvous with Paulinus could have put the remaining soldiers in danger of annihilation. It is very unlikely that Postumus would have disobeyed a direct order. The only alternative could have been to abandon its fort in Exeter entirely, which might mean that the whole of the south-west would be lost to local tribes.

British rebels, who were lying in wait for whoever dared to travel to and from the II legion's fort, may have intercepted any messengers riding in and out of the fort. Indeed, Posthumus and his men may not have received the order at all. The life expectancy of Roman messenger riders could be questionable. If they were ever caught by marauding militia in hostile country, their severed heads would become yet more trophies, and their remains fed to the hunting dogs. This is why it is vitally important for any fort commander to carry out constant patrols around their camps to ensure any insurgents do not establish themselves within striking distance of the fort or be a threat to the fort's supply lines. Considering that Posthumus was third in command it is tragic that he retains the blame for the Legion's lack of response.

Of all the many unanswered questions about the aftermath of the battle. The biggest mystery is what happened to Boudicca herself. Tacitus claims that Boudicca "ended her life with poison", while Dio merely writes that Boudicca "fell ill and died" at about the time of the battle. She was given a "lavish funeral" soon afterwards before her followers "disbanded in the belief that now they really were defeated". The fate of Boudicca's two daughters is not mentioned at all, even though they were said to have ridden in their mother's chariot on the battlefield. It is doubtful that Boudicca poisoned herself or died of illness at the time of the battle. If she had died, the Romans would have wanted to seize her body and display it as a trophy to warn others as they often did with vanquished foes. The claim that she died of disease, or committed suicide, may be Roman propaganda, intended to provide "closure" to her story, and to stop her appearing like a heroic martyr, fighting to the last. If Boudicca had died in battle, or been slaughtered after being captured, or surrendering, it is surprising that her body then disappeared. Given her striking appearance and her gender (there are no other references to women on the battlefield itself), it would be unlikely that her body would escape identification. Dio's writings do include quite a detailed description of Boudicca even though it is almost certainly a fabrication:

In stature she was very tall, in appearance most terrifying, in the glance of her eye most fierce, and her voice was harsh; 4 a great mass of the tawniest hair fell to her hips; around her neck was a large golden necklace; and she wore a tunic of divers colours over which a thick mantle was fastened with a brooch.

There have been several claims that Boudicca fled to Wales with her daughters, and that she spent the rest of her life there. Indeed, Boudicca and her daughters could have quite possibly been hurried away quickly before Romans got to her. This theory is credible. Welsh folklore has long maintained that Boudicca ended up in Wales, and some Welsh historians have claimed that she began her revolt to avenge Paulinus's slaughter of Welsh Druids. There is some evidence of contact between eastern British tribes and the Silures of South Wales. Caractacus, a chieftain of the Catuvellauni tribe, fought against the Romans alongside the Silures before being defeated by Scapula in 50AD.

If Boudicca did escape alive, the Roman embarrassment would have been considerable. Rome did not allow leaders of rebellions to escape easily: it normally pursued them to the edges of the known world. Vercingetorix suffered a humiliating death, being imprisoned in the Tullianum in Rome for nearly six years before being publicly paraded, ceremonially strangled and then beheaded. It is likely that Boudicca would have met a similar fate had she been captured alive. The earlier British rebel, Caractacus had been spared, having fled to the territory of Queen Cartimandua, queen of the Brigantes (a tribe in present-day Yorkshire and Cumbria), who handed him over to the Romans. Caractacus was taken back to Rome and sentenced to death, but, apparently he made a speech that persuaded the emperor Claudius to spare him, and he was allowed to live in Rome for the rest of his life. This is unlikely, firstly, he would have only spoken ancient Brittonic, which the Romans would not have been able to understand. Secondly, he was instrumental in the killings of hundreds of Roman legionnaires during his campaigns against his Roman oppressors which lasted for over nine years. It is unlikely that he would have been spared, the story is just more propaganda for the benefit of the Roman readers. If the Romans did try to find Boudicca after the battle, they clearly never succeeded. If she did escape to Wales, she had managed to humiliate the Romans twice: firstly, by almost wrestling control of Britain from them, and secondly by escaping their violent revenge.

Burial mounds at the top of the defile

8

Conclusion

Resolving the question of where Boudicca's army was defeated matters. The battle was a turning point, if not *the* turning point, of early British history. If the Romans had lost the battle, they would have been forced to leave the British Isles for good, never to return. The Roman occupation of Britain would have been a historical blip, not centuries-long. The dark ages would have started sooner and perhaps be a lot darker. The flames of the Boudiccan rebellion have been remembered since the late 16th century and affected the course of British history ever since. Paradoxically, it could be argued that by losing two out of the four legions at Paulinus' disposal prior to the battle could quite possibly have increased his chances. Should all the 4 legions have been with him at the start of the uprising he may have chosen a different place other than the Pascombe escarpment as the battleground. Accordingly, the outcome could have been completely different.

Waite has argued that if Boudicca had won, she would not have been the queen of a united Britain for long, and that its tribes would have soon started fighting each other again. Maybe the most important consequences would have been cultural and linguistic. Today we would know a lot less about the centuries that followed, as no document written in Old English has been found from earlier than around 600AD; the only other source of events in Britain before then are Roman documents, written in Latin and Greek. If Britain had not had a Roman occupation until about 420AD it would not have got in the habit of writing things down. Britain might have turned out to be more like Ireland, a country whose native language has little in common with Latin, and which had a stronger tradition of oral history, not history that is recorded.

By winning the battle the Romans cemented their power over what we now call England. The only serious uprisings against the Romans in the three centuries that followed were on the northern fringes of Britannia, in what we now call Scotland, and on the western fringes, in what we now call Wales. As Tacitus wrote, "the favourable outcome of a single battle restored the province to its old submission".

Boudicca's uprising, and its defeat, may also be the main reason why London became the capital city. Colchester remained the capital of Roman Britain until the end of the first century, but its decline had begun with its sacking in 61AD. London's destruction had been less total, and gradually London overtook Colchester in size, and become the capital of Britannia in the 2nd century. London has been the capital of England, and later Great Britain, almost continuously ever since. It could be argued that London's primacy really began after Boudicca's defeat, when the Romans decided that Londinium was a better strategic location. Had Boudicca not rebelled, or had her rebellion been victorious, it is possible that Colchester may never have been toppled as the largest and most important settlement in Britain, and it might even still be our capital today.

For Britons who were opposed to the Roman occupation, the Boudiccan uprising was the "end of the road", Graham Webster has argued. "The year AD 60 was a watershed for many Britons, since up to this moment there was a real possibility that somehow the Roman government might be persuaded to give up its conquest". Webster saw the uprising as a counter-colonial uprising analogous to the Mau-Mau rebellion in Kenya in the 1950s, or the troubles in Northern Ireland from 1969 onwards. Later generations of Britons learned to live with the Roman Peace - "Pax Romana" and assimilated, rather than seek to overthrow it. They were later seen as the *nouveau riche* of the northern Roman empire, who accepted the economic benefits of Roman rule more readily than most other peoples that the Romans had conquered.

Given that the battle was such a key moment in our islands' story, it is now vital that archaeology catches up, and that there is a detailed excavation in and around Pascombe Hill. As Graham Webster once wrote, "The site of the great battle which decided the fate of Roman Britain will never be known for certain, unless some quite remarkable finds are made, such as a mass burial with closely identifiable weapons in association". Although battlefields have often been extensively looted, there should be enough to help archaeologists in their quest at the hill and the plain at its base. If Pascombe Hill was indeed where 80,000 Britons lost their lives, there should be many objects such as arrow heads, slingshot, knives, swords and armour lying underground. There should be evidence of animal husbandry, such as bridle bits and ironwork from the wagons, and bits of pottery that could be attributed to the Celtic tribes fallen from their baggage train. Above all, there will be human, and animal remains that could be carbon-dated. Bones with wounds inflicted by sharp objects, such as swords, would provide the necessary proof that this is indeed the battlefield. If a bucket-full of slingshot is found at Pascombe Hill, we're there. Unfortunately, if extensive investigation does not take place officially, the area will be subject to an abundance of unauthorised treasure hunters looking for historical artifacts to detrimental effect.

Any visitor to the Dunstable Downs escarpment can easily experience how difficult it would have been for the Celts to climb Pascombe Hill. Anyone who tries to climb the steep, grassy slopes soon realises that they have made a mistake. It looks easy, even inviting, but it is very challenging to make it to the top. Charging against an army positioned halfway up the slope in the defensive *Phalanx* formation was a fatal blunder, that easily resulted in the complete annihilation of Boudicca's Celtic forces. It is easy to see how the Romans could have used this narrow defile with a 360-degree view from the top, to defeat a much larger British force. It is obvious that this site is much closer to Tacitus's description than any of the other places that have been suggested to date.

It is disappointing that such an age-old scheduled monument such as the Five Knolls barrow cemetery at the top of the defile is used as tracks for mountain bikers and walkers; which, you will agree is not very respectful, but the cyclists and pedestrians may have no idea that they may be crossing over ancient burial mounds dating back to the neolithic and may have the remains of Roman soldiers from one of the most important battles in ancient British history. Margaret Hughes once wrote about Boudicca's army: "Nowhere in Britain is there any memorial to the fallen... This battle - so decisive in the history of this island - deserves to be commemorated and appreciated somewhere. Therefore, we owe it to the fallen of Boudicca's immense army to find the site and give closure to an event that secured British history indefinitely. If Pascombe Hill is ever confirmed as the battle site, it should be treated with the same reverence as Avebury, Creswell Crags, Hastings, Stonehenge, Maiden Castle, and Skara Brae to name but a few.

As Dio puts it: 'So much for the affairs in Britain.'

[i] The 1995 film *Braveheart* wrongly portrayed medieval Scottish warriors drenched in blue woad, but the practice was in fact only common hundreds of years earlier, on the bodies of Celtic tribesman across Britain.

[ii] The Romans called their battle lines *acies, referring* to the cutting edge of their sword blades. As well as a simple line of soldiers - *simplex acies* – Caesar often used the *duplex acies*, but his preferred choice seemed to be the *triplex acies:* three rows of infantry.

[iii] Dio says that Boudicca amassed an army of 120,000 troops to begin with, and that by the time of the final battle it had grown to 230,000: if these figures are to be believed, as well as Tacitus's claim that 80,000 of them were killed in the final battle, that means that between and one and two thirds of the British army was annihilated at the Battle of Watling Street. It may have been an even higher proportion than two-thirds, given that some of the British would have been lost in earlier operations.

[iv] Evidence of a Roman amphitheatre has been discovered less than a hundred metres from the place where the skulls were discovered, which gives weight to this theory. The slain combatants could have been placed in a burial pit adjacent to the site, and their remains could have eventually seeped in to the Walbrook over the centuries.

See https://www.museumoflondon.org.uk/discover /gladiator -games-roman -gladiators-londinium.

Bibliography

Keith Branigan	The Catuvellauni	Alan Sutton Publishing	1985
Rosalind Dunnett	The Trinovantes	Duckworth Press	1975
Charles Rivers Editors	Boudica	Charles Rivers Editors	2022
Vanessa Collingridge	Boudica –	Ebury Press -	2005
Cowan R	Roman Battle Tactics		
109BC – AD 3134	Osprey Publishing		2007
Davies J	The Land of the Iceni	Oxbow Books	1999
De La Bédoyére G	Gladius	Little, Brown	2020
De La Bédoyére G	Defying Rome.	The History Press	2003
The Rebels of Roman Britain	Tempus Stroud		2003
Dio C	The Roman History	Penguin Classics	1987
Fraser A	The Warrior Queens	Phoenix	2002
Gilliver C	Military Strategy	Tempus	1999
Higgins C	Journeys in Roman Britain	Vintage Books	2014
Roger Nolan	Julius Caesar's Invasion of Britain	Frontline Books	2018
Neil Oliver	A history of Ancient Britain	Weidenfeld & Nicolson	2012
Alice Roberts	The Celts	Heron Books	2015
Janet Smart	Boudicca the Truth	Self Publishing Partner	2022
Cornelius Tacitus	The Agricola	Penguin Classics	1970
Cornelius Tacitus –	The Annals and Histories	Random House	2003
John Waite –	Boudica's Last Stand	The History Press	2007
G. Webster	The British Revolt against Rome	Routledge	1978
Michael Wood –	In Search of the Dark Ages	BBC Books	2005

Peter Sweeney

References:

Fuentes N.	*Boudica Revisted*	London	1985
Hughes M	The Mancetter Candidacy	academia.edu	2013
Steve Kaye	Finding the site of Boudica's last battle	banddarchaeology	2013
Brewer R	*CAER Rufeinig Gelligaer Roman Fort*	Gelligaer & Pen-y-Bryn	
S. Ireland	A Source Book	Routledge	1996

Classical Sources:

Cassius Dio	*The Roman Histories*	Penguin Classics	*1987*
Julius Caesar	*The Gallic Wars*	*Enhanced Media*	*2016*
Pliny the Elder	*Natural History*	*Penquin Classics*	*1991*

Websites:

www.academia.edu

www.archaeologyuk.org

www.bandaarchaeologyphysics.co.uk

www.englishmonarchs.co.uk

www.forgottenbooks.com

www.icknieldwaytrail.org.uk

www.londonist.com/is-boudica-buried-in-london

www.museumoflondon.org.uk

www.nationaltrust.or.uk

90

www.rentaroman.co.uk

www.roman-britain.org

www.silburycoins.co.uk

www.viridor-doinghistory.co.uk

www.wikepedia.org

www.ranker.com

INDEX

Milton Keynes UK
Ingram Content Group UK Ltd.
UKHW050312110124
435803UK00001B/3